THE TRUTH ABOUT
MEGHAN

THE LITERARY BIOGRAPHY

THE TRUTH ABOUT
MEGHAN

ROWAN LOWRY

STANDARD
CANDLE
PRESS

A STANDARD CANDLE PAPERBACK

First published in the UK in 2026
by Standard Candle Press
email: info@standardcandlepress.uk

This book is a work of non-fiction based on public records, legal
documents, broadcast interviews, published journalism, and the
subjects' own accounts. Where dialogue appears, it is reconstructed
from documented sources. The author has made every effort to ensure
accuracy but makes no warranty regarding completeness.

This is an unauthorised biography. The author has no affiliation with
the British Royal Family or any member of the Sussex household.

ISBN: 978-1-9195374-0-5

Printed and bound by Ingram Content Group

Contents

"Prince Harry is worried about Ms Markle's safety and is
deeply disappointed that he has not been able to protect her"
Kensington Palace statement, 8 November 2016

Prologue

The engines were already warming when Meghan stepped onto the aircraft, the cold air of the runway following her inside. She paused at the top of the stairs because her breath caught unexpectedly. The sky above RAF Northolt was its usual London grey, tight and low, the kind of sky that pressed down rather than opened up. She'd lived under that sky for years now. She had tried to make peace with it. But tonight it felt different. Heavy. Watching. She climbed the last steps and ducked into the cabin.

Inside, the lights were dim, the sort of soft illumination designed to make travel feel private even when nothing about the moment felt private. Meghan moved down the narrow aisle, Archie warm against her chest, his small fingers curled into the fabric of her coat. He was too young to understand why they were leaving at this hour, why his mother's hands trembled slightly as she settled into the window seat, why his father kept looking back towards the door as if expecting someone to stop them. He only knew he was tired and that his favourite toy was in his bag and that the aeroplane made interesting sounds. She envied him that. The pure simplicity of not knowing.

She handed him carefully to the flight attendant, a woman with a quiet, practised smile who didn't ask questions, who simply took the boy and murmured something soothing. Meghan watched her son's face as he was carried towards the small sleeping area at the back. He didn't cry. He rarely cried anymore. She wondered sometimes if he'd absorbed some of the tension that filled their days, learned already to hold things in.

Harry was still at the front of the cabin, speaking to the pilot in low tones. His posture was familiar to her now in all its variations, and this one she knew well. Shoulders braced, jaw set, the careful control of a man who had spent his whole life being watched and had learned to give nothing away. But she could read what others couldn't. The exhaustion beneath the composure. The grief he wouldn't name.

He finished with the pilot and walked back towards her, and when he sat down his hand found hers immediately, an instinct now, the way they anchored each other through everything.

The door closed.

The sound was solid, hollow, final. Meghan felt it in her stomach. She thought of Frogmore Cottage, the home they'd barely had time to make theirs. The nursery they'd painted themselves, the two of them in old clothes, laughing at nothing, believing things would get easier. The garden where she'd planned to plant vegetables in spring. Small dreams. Ordinary dreams. The kind that weren't supposed to be too much to ask.

She placed her hand against the oval of the window. The glass was colder than she expected. Beyond it, the ground crew moved in slow, methodical arcs, their neon jackets glowing against the darkness. One of them glanced up at the aircraft, and she pulled back instinctively, though she knew he couldn't see her through the tinted glass. The instinct to hide had become automatic. Another thing she'd learned here.

Harry squeezed her hand. "We can still turn back."

She looked at him. They both knew it wasn't true. There was nothing to turn back to. The institution had made that clear enough. Half measures weren't acceptable. Compromise wasn't possible. They'd offered everything they could think of, every arrangement that might let them serve and survive at the same time, and the answer had been the same each time. All or nothing. Stay and diminish, or go and be free.

"I know," she said anyway. Because she understood why he'd said it. Because even now, even after everything, part of him was still looking for a way to keep both worlds.

The engines tightened their pitch. The cabin vibrated. Through the window, the runway lights began to slide past, then blur, white and amber streaking into speed.

Meghan thought of the headlines that would come tomorrow. She could write them herself by now. 'Meghan flees Britain'. 'Duchess abandons duty'. Harry's wife tears him from his family. They would say she had changed him, ruined him, stolen him away. They would not say that he had made a choice. That he had looked at what staying would cost and decided his wife and son were worth more than a title, more than a palace, more than the approval of people who had never tried to know him.

They would not say that she had begged him to stay, once. That she had offered to disappear quietly, to let him keep his life while she rebuilt hers somewhere far away. That he had looked at her with something close to anger and said, If you think I would let you go through this alone, you don't know me at all.

The wheels left the ground.

A soft jolt. A tilt. The familiar weightlessness.

Meghan felt the small surrender of gravity, and for one suspended moment she imagined she could leave it all on the runway below. The noise, the scrutiny, the unrelenting weight of being visible to millions who had decided she was the villain in a story she had never auditioned for.

Beneath them, London tilted and fell away. The lights of the city, millions of them, became indistinguishable from one another, just a glow against the dark, no longer separating into palaces and tabloid offices and the hospital where she had wanted to end everything. Just light. Just a place she had lived. Just somewhere she was leaving.

She closed her eyes. The cabin hummed around her, small and enclosed and safe. She thought of arriving in this country years ago, how nervous she had been, how full of hope. She had believed she could do some good here. Believed the institution might bend enough to let her be useful, let her be herself. She had been wrong about that. But she had been right about Harry. Right to trust him, right to love him, right to believe that when everything else failed, he would still be beside her.

"You okay?"

His voice was low, almost lost beneath the engine noise.

She turned to look at him. His eyes were red-rimmed, though he would never admit to crying. His hand in hers was warm and steady and sure.

"I'm tired," she said. "But I'm okay."

He nodded. He didn't ask anything else. There would be time for talking later, for processing, for grief and relief and whatever came after. For now, it was enough to sit together while the plane carried them through the darkness.

Meghan leant her head against his shoulder and let herself exhale fully for the first time in months. Maybe years. The sky outside the window dimmed from grey to black, the last of the clouds falling away beneath them until there was nothing but stars and the distant curve of the earth and the steady hum of engines carrying them forward.

She didn't know what waited on the other side of this flight. She knew only that staying had become impossible, and that leaving was the first honest thing she had done in longer than she could remember.

The world above the storm was quiet.

She closed her eyes, and let it hold her.

**"Miss Markle's mother is a dreadlocked African-American
lady from the wrong side of the tracks"**
Rachel Johnson, *Mail on Sunday*, 6 November 2016

1

'Mixed Signals'

The classroom had a form that needed filling in. Standard stuff for a Los Angeles elementary school in the early 1990s, boxes to tick about ethnicity and race so the district could track demographics and funding. The teacher handed them out during morning registration, explaining that students should check the box that best described them.

Meghan looked at the options. White. Black. Hispanic. Asian. Pacific Islander. Other. The boxes sat there in neat rows, waiting to categorise her into something simple. She read them again, as if reading more carefully might reveal one she'd missed. A box that said both. A box that said my mother is black and my father is white and I am all of these things at once. But there was no such box. There was only the neat grid, the single expectation, the silent insistence that she be one thing or another.

She raised her hand. "Miss, what if you're more than one?"

The teacher glanced up from her desk. "Just pick the one that fits best."

"But I'm black and white. My mum's black, my dad's white. Which box do I use?"

The other children had stopped working. Meghan felt their attention like a weight, all those eyes trying to solve the puzzle of her. Some of them knew her parents, had been to her house for birthday parties, understood that families could look different from the television version. Others were trying to figure out what she was, why she didn't look like one thing or another, why she was making this complicated. A boy two rows over squinted at her as if seeing her for the first time. She looked down at her desk.

The teacher walked over, looked at the form, then at Meghan. "You can leave it blank if you want."

"But then it looks like I didn't do it properly."

"Then pick one. It doesn't really matter."

But it did matter. Meghan couldn't have explained why, not then, not in words a teacher would understand. It mattered because choosing one meant erasing the other. Choosing white meant her mother didn't count. Choosing black meant her father didn't count. Either way, half of her would disappear into that little box, and she would walk out of this classroom as something less than what she'd walked in as.

She left it blank.

That afternoon, she took the form home and showed it to her mother, explaining the problem. Doria sat at the kitchen table, the form between them, and was quiet for a long moment. The light through the window was warm and golden, the kind of Los Angeles light that made everything look hopeful. But her mother's face was serious, thoughtful, carrying a weight Meghan didn't fully understand yet.

"You don't have to choose," Doria said finally.

"Don't let anyone tell you that you have to be one thing when you're both."

"But the form only has one box."

"Then the form is wrong."

Doria called the school the next morning. Meghan listened from the hallway, her back against the wall, cereal going soggy in the bowl she'd abandoned on the counter. Her mother's voice stayed calm and firm as she explained that forcing a child to deny half her heritage wasn't acceptable. There was a long pause. Then Doria said, "I understand it's how the form has always been. That doesn't mean it's how the form should be."

Another pause. Meghan held her breath.

"Thank you," Doria said. "I appreciate that."

She hung up and found Meghan in the hallway. "They're going to add a box," she said. "For people who are more than one thing."

Meghan didn't say anything. She just hugged her mother, pressing her face into the familiar softness of Doria's sweater, with a feeling she couldn't name. Relief, maybe. Or something bigger. The understanding that the world could be wrong, and that a single voice could make it change.

The television studio smelled like coffee and sawdust and something electrical that Meghan never could identify. She'd spent dozens of Saturdays here watching her father work, sitting in corners with her homework while he adjusted lights and checked angles and made television shows look real. Thomas Markle was a lighting director on *Married... with Children* and *General Hospital*, an Emmy winner for his work on the soap, respected by crews and actors who understood that lighting was half of what made a scene work.

Meghan loved watching him. The way he moved through the set with purpose, making tiny adjustments that most people wouldn't notice but that changed everything. A light tilted two degrees. A gel changed from amber to blue. Shadows falling across a face differently. The actors would say their lines the same way, but suddenly you believed them more, or less, depending on what her father had done.

"Why do you move that light so much?" she asked him once, during a break. They were sitting on folding chairs near the craft services table, sharing a packet of crisps.

"Because the actor's face needs to tell the story. If the light's wrong, you don't see what they're feeling."

"So you're making them look different?"

"I'm making them look like themselves. There's a difference."

She thought about that for a long time after. The idea that what you saw on screen wasn't just reality captured, but reality constructed. Someone decided how to light the scene, which angle to shoot from, what to show and what to hide. Someone decided which faces got lit properly and which faded into background. It was a kind of power, she realised. Invisible, but real.

Her father let her stand beside him sometimes while he worked, explaining what he was doing in quiet tones that wouldn't disturb the actors. She learned the vocabulary. Key light, fill light, backlight. Hard shadows, soft shadows. The way a single bulb could transform someone from villain to hero depending on where you placed it.

"Everyone thinks acting is the hard part," Thomas told her once. "But the actor can do everything right and still look wrong if the lighting doesn't support them. My job is to make sure the audience sees what they're supposed to see."

What they're supposed to see. Meghan filed that away.

One afternoon, Doria picked her up from school and sensed immediately that something had happened. Meghan sat quietly in the passenger seat, arms folded in the way she had when she was trying not to cry.

A teacher had divided the class by race for an activity, something about cultural heritage presentations, and Meghan had been told to pick a side.

She was nine.

She had stood in the middle of the classroom while other children filed obediently to their designated corners, and she hadn't known where to go.

"Pick one," the teacher had said, impatient.

"But I'm both."

"You can't be both. Just pick the one you feel more connected to."

She had gone to the black students' corner, because her mother was the one who picked her up from school, her mother was the one who braided her hair, her mother was the one she saw every day. But walking across that classroom had felt like betrayal. Like leaving her father behind.

Doria didn't give a lecture when Meghan finally explained what had happened. She just drove to the beach. They stepped out into the late-afternoon salt air, the sky the colour of fresh apricots, the waves making their patient rhythm against the sand. Meghan watched the tide bring in small foamy curls. The water didn't care what colour anyone was. It just moved the way it had always moved, indifferent to the categories humans invented.

Doria knelt beside her and said, "You don't have to choose."

"You said that before. About the form."

"I'll keep saying it until you believe it."

California is often described in clichés. Sunshine, palm trees, promises. But the California Meghan grew up in was stranger and more contradictory than that. In the early 1980s, Los Angeles was a collection of mosaics pretending to be a single city. Streets changed flavour in a single turn. A few blocks one way, wealth. A few blocks the other, gritty storefronts, cracked pavements, the glow of families making do. She moved between them with ease.

Her parents made sure of that. Doria and Thomas lived in the sort of quiet orbit ex-partners develop when the breakup doesn't destroy the friendship underneath. Meghan moved between households as if crossing stages between scenes. Different lighting, different props, same core character. Doria's home had jazz humming through open windows and a sense of flow. Thomas's house was quieter, more structured, television always on, scripts stacked on tables. Both parents loved her completely. Neither expected her to pick sides or declare loyalty. They'd failed at marriage but succeeded at divorce, which was its own kind of achievement.

The commercial appeared during after-school programming, a dish soap advertisement that opened with a woman scrubbing pots as the voice-over announced, "Women all over America are fighting greasy pots and pans."

Meghan was eleven, sitting on the sofa in her mother's apartment, doing homework with the television on for background noise. The words landed wrong, made her stop mid-sentence in her maths problem.

Women all over America are fighting greasy pots and pans.

Not people. Women. As if cleaning dishes was naturally women's work, as if men couldn't be bothered with domestic labour, as if an entire gender existed primarily to fight grease. She thought about her father, who cooked and cleaned in his house when she stayed with him. She thought about her mother, who worked full-time and still handled all the household management. The commercial wasn't just annoying. It was lying about the world.

She mentioned it at school the next day, during a discussion about current events that the teacher had loosely organised around whatever was in the news. "I saw this commercial that said women fight greasy pots and pans. Like it's our job just because we're women."

Some kids laughed. Others looked confused. One boy said, "Well, my mum does the dishes."

"So does mine. But so does my dad when I'm at his place. It's not a women thing, it's a people thing."

The teacher, sensing an actual teaching moment, suggested they write letters. Companies responded to consumer feedback, she explained. If something bothered you, you could say so. Most of the class ignored the assignment or wrote halfhearted complaints about breakfast cereals with too much sugar.

Meghan took it seriously. She sat at her desk that evening with her best stationery, the kind with flowers along the border that her grandmother had given her, and wrote to Procter & Gamble, the company behind the dish soap. She explained, in careful handwriting, that their commercial was sexist and should be changed. She wrote to Gloria Allred, the feminist lawyer she'd seen on television talking about women's rights. She wrote to the then First Lady, Hillary Clinton.

She didn't expect responses. She just knew staying quiet felt like accepting something she disagreed with. But responses came. Hillary Clinton's office wrote back, encouraging her to keep speaking up. *Nick News* invited her to appear on their programme, an eleven-year-old explaining why words mattered, why "women" and "people" weren't interchangeable.

Six weeks later, a letter arrived. Procter & Gamble were changing the commercial. From "women all over America" to "people all over America." A single word. A tiny change that mattered.

Meghan read the letter three times, standing in the kitchen with the envelope still in her hand. Then she brought it to school, showed it to her teacher. The teacher made a copy and put it on the bulletin board. See what can happen when you speak up, she wrote underneath.

Meghan looked at that letter on the bulletin board and thought about her mother calling the school about the form. About the new box that now existed because someone had insisted it should. About voices, and whether they mattered, and what happened when you used yours.

She joined the drama programme at secondary school because it seemed like something she might be good at. Memorising lines, embodying characters, making audiences believe you were someone else. It connected to what she'd learnt watching her father work, the idea that performance could reveal truth if you did it right.

She wasn't the most talented actor in her class. Some kids had an instinct she didn't, a looseness, a willingness to throw themselves into emotion without worrying how it looked. But she was reliable. She showed up prepared, took direction well, didn't fall apart when things went wrong during performances.

One teacher pulled her aside after a particularly difficult scene during rehearsal. They were doing *Our Town*, and Meghan had been cast as Emily, who dies young and returns to watch her own life with unbearable clarity. The scene should have broken the audience's heart. It hadn't.

"You're very controlled," the teacher said. "Almost too controlled. Good acting requires vulnerability."

Meghan nodded. She understood what the teacher meant, but she didn't know how to access it. Control had been survival. At school, at home, moving between worlds that didn't quite fit together. You held yourself carefully. You didn't give people ammunition to use against you later. You maintained composure.

But acting required the opposite. You had to be willing to be seen failing, struggling, falling apart. You had to trust that showing weakness wouldn't destroy you.

She worked on it. Slowly, carefully, learning to let cracks show during performances, to trust that audiences wanted real emotion, not perfect presentation. The performances that landed hardest were the ones where she stopped protecting herself and just existed as the character, flaws and needs and failures all visible.

It felt dangerous every time. And every time, it worked.

She packed her small suitcase and prepared to leave for Northwestern University, boarding a plane to Chicago with a notebook in her bag and California sun still on her skin. She didn't know exactly what she wanted. She knew only that she wanted more than the boxes the world kept offering her. More than the single tick box. More than the corners of rooms she was supposed to stand in.

She wanted to be seen fully. To be known as all of herself at once. She didn't know yet how rarely the world allowed that. But she was going to try anyway.

"Meghan Markle was a Deal or No Deal briefcase girl"
Rosaleen Fenton, *Daily Mirror*, 26 June 2021

2

'Deal or No Deal'

Evanston, Illinois hit Meghan like climate shock that first September. She'd grown up under perpetual sun. Now she stood on a campus where autumn actually meant something. Leaves turning colours she'd only seen in photographs, air carrying a chill that required layers she didn't own yet. Northwestern stretched along Lake Michigan, Gothic buildings and modern architecture existing in uneasy harmony. The theatre programme was housed in a complex that smelled like sawdust, makeup, and decades of ambition. Meghan loved it immediately.

The double major meant brutal course loads. Theatre and international relations. Mornings spent analysing Chekhov, afternoons dissecting foreign policy. Her classmates thought the combination was strange.

"What are you going to do with that?" someone asked during orientation week.

Meghan shrugged. "I don't know yet. But understanding how people feel and why they feel it seems useful."

The theatre programme was competitive in ways that surprised her. Everyone had been the star of their school drama department.

Everyone had talent. The question was who had discipline, who could take direction, who could fail repeatedly without losing hunger. Meghan watched her classmates audition for the same roles she wanted, watched some of them land parts that should have been hers, watched others flame out entirely when the pressure became too much. She wasn't the best. But she was still standing.

One professor, a former Broadway actor named Vincent, pulled her aside after a particularly difficult scene study class. They were in one of the small rehearsal rooms, afternoon light slanting through high windows, dust motes suspended in the air. Meghan knew what was coming. The same feedback she'd heard in high school. Too controlled. Not loose enough. Trying too hard.

"You're not a natural," Vincent said.

The words landed exactly where she'd expected them to, in the place that had been waiting for confirmation. She wasn't good enough. She'd known it all along.

"That's not an insult," Vincent continued, watching her face. "Sit down. Let me explain something."

She sat. He pulled a chair opposite her, leaning forward with his elbows on his knees.

"Naturals plateau," he said. "They rely on instinct, and instinct only takes you so far. When the material gets difficult, when the role requires something they've never felt, they don't know how to get there. They've never had to learn. You're different. You're a builder. You construct performances brick by brick, moment by moment. It's slower. It's harder. But it means you can go anywhere, play anything, because you know how to build what you don't naturally have."

Meghan absorbed this. "So being bad at instinct is actually..."

"It's actually your advantage. As long as you keep building."

She held onto that assessment like a life raft during the inevitable rejections that would follow. You're a builder.

When casting didn't go her way, when directors chose some-one else, when she sat alone in her dorm room wondering if she was wasting her time, she'd hear Vincent's voice. Brick by brick. That'll take you further in the long run.

The college years passed in a blur of rehearsals and research papers, late nights in the library and later nights in black box the-atres, friendships formed over shared exhaustion and cheap pizza. She joined Alpha Kappa Alpha, her mother's sorority, finding community amongst black women who understood the particular pressures of excelling in predominantly white institutions. Women who didn't need her to explain why she sometimes felt like she was performing a version of herself for white classmates, or why certain comments landed wrong even when they weren't meant to hurt.

The summer after her sophomore year, she secured an intern-ship at the US Embassy in Buenos Aires. She wanted to under-stand how diplomacy actually worked on the ground, how policy translated into practice, how power moved through rooms where everyone smiled while they pursued conflicting agendas.

Buenos Aires was intoxicating. European architecture with Latin American energy, political tension simmering beneath café culture, tango in the streets and protests in the plaza. She shared an apartment with two other interns, practised her Spanish on patient locals, learnt to navigate a city where clocks ran differ-ently than in California or Chicago.

The embassy work was mostly administrative. Filing, schedul-ing, drafting memos that would be rewritten by senior staff. But she observed everything. How diplomats spoke differently in public versus private. How information moved through hier-archies. How power operated through implication rather than declaration.

One evening, at a diplomatic reception, she watched an am-bassador navigate a conversation between representatives from countries with hostile relations. He smiled, made jokes, kept the tone light. And somehow, by the end, they'd agreed to a meeting that had seemed impossible an hour earlier. She approached him later, glass of wine in hand, curious.

"How did you do that?"

The ambassador glanced at her, seeming to weigh whether she was genuinely interested or just making conversation. "Make them feel seen," he said finally. "People will compromise on policy if they feel respected personally. Most conflicts are about dignity, not just positions." She filed that away.

Returning to Northwestern for junior year, Meghan threw herself fully into theatre. She performed in student productions, took on challenging roles, studied actors she admired. Meryl Streep's chameleon transformations, Audrey Hepburn's grace under scrutiny, Sidney Poitier's dignified power.

She was cast as Sally Bowles in *Cabaret*, a role that required her to be sexually confident, emotionally messy, performative yet vulnerable. Sally was a woman who performed happiness so convincingly that she almost believed it herself, who fell apart only when the audience caught glimpses of what she was hiding. The director pushed Meghan hard.

"You're too controlled," he'd say during rehearsals. "Sally's falling apart. I need to see the cracks."

Meghan struggled with that direction. Control had always been her protection. You didn't show people the messy parts. You didn't let them see you failing. But Sally required the opposite. Sally required her to stand on stage and let the audience watch her unravel.

Opening night, something clicked. She walked onto the stage for Sally's final number, and instead of performing desperation, she simply stopped holding herself together. She let the exhaustion show. The fear. The knowledge that the world Sally had built was collapsing and there was nothing she could do to stop it. The applause afterwards felt different than any she'd received before. Like recognition.

Vincent found her backstage, his eyes bright with satisfaction.

"There you are," he said. "That's what I've been waiting to see."

By senior year, the future pressed in with uncomfortable urgency. Her classmates were making plans. Grad school, law school, moving to New York, accepting corporate jobs that offered security if not passion. Meghan knew she wanted to act, but wanting wasn't a plan.

Her father urged caution over the phone. "Have a backup," Thomas said. "The industry's brutal. Most actors never work."

She knew he was right. The statistics were devastating. Ninety percent unemployment at any given time. Decades of training for careers that might never materialise. She understood the logic of having something to fall back on. But she also knew that fallback plans had a way of becoming primary plans, that safety nets could become cages.

Doria, when Meghan called her with the same news, responded differently.

"Do it," she said simply.

"That's it? No warnings?"

"Baby, you're going to do it anyway. I'm just supporting the inevitable."

Graduation came in June 2003. Meghan returned to Los Angeles with a degree, a few hundred dollars, and a resolve that felt both sturdy and fragile. She moved into a small apartment in Hollywood. The gritty part where rent was manageable and sirens were frequent, not the glamorous part where movie premieres happened and celebrities ate lunch.

The apartment was a studio with a Murphy bed that didn't quite fold correctly and a kitchenette that required creative contortion to use. But it was hers. The windows faced east, catching morning light. She hung photos from Northwestern, bought plants that would die and be replaced, set up a corner desk for the journals she still kept.

She'd saved head-shots from a photographer in Chicago. Professional enough to look serious, affordable enough not to drain her savings. She made copies, assembled packets with her resumé listing theatre credits no casting director would care about, and began the ritual every actor knows. Opening *Backstage* magazine, circling auditions, preparing for rejection.

The first auditions were humbling. She'd wait in rooms filled with women who looked like her, or nothing like her, or exactly like whoever had been cast in last week's successful pilot. The energy was performative even before anyone read. Forced confidence, calculated friendliness, the constant assessment of who posed a threat.

Meghan tried different strategies. Being warm and approachable. Being aloof and mysterious. Being exactly what she thought they wanted. None of it worked consistently.

The feedback, when it came, was coded.

"Not right for this role."

"We're going in a different direction."

"Loved your audition but..."

The "but" never led anywhere useful. The real reasons stayed hidden behind polite deflection.

One audition stayed with her. A sitcom pilot about roommates in New York. She walked into the room, smiled, introduced herself. The casting director glanced up, looked at her head-shot, looked at her again. His expression betrayed his thoughts, and he said it anyway.

"You're more... ethnic than I expected."

Meghan blinked. "I'm sorry?"

"From the photo. I just." He waved his hand vaguely. "We're looking for someone who reads more clearly."

She understood immediately what clearly meant. Someone whose race was obvious at a glance. Someone who could be easily categorised, filed into a box, cast without confusion. Someone who wasn't whatever she was.

She finished the audition professionally. She smiled, thanked them for the opportunity, walked out through the waiting room where other women sat hoping for their chance. She made it to her car before the shaking started. She sat in the driver's seat with her hands on the wheel, not crying, just sitting, trying to understand what had just happened.

She had been too much of something. Or not enough of something else. She wasn't clear. And there was nothing she could do about it, no amount of preparation or training that could make her face read the way they wanted it to read.

Another casting director, months later, asked if her hair could be straightened. "It's just a lot," he said, gesturing vaguely at her curls. "For television, you know. Simpler is better."

She straightened her hair for the next few auditions. It didn't help. The "ethnic" label followed her regardless of how she styled herself.

Acting alone couldn't pay rent. Meghan cycled through the jobs that kept struggling actors afloat. Catering events where she served hors d'oeuvres to industry executives who didn't see her. Working as a freelance calligrapher, those Immaculate Heart nuns having taught her something marketable after all. She addressed wedding invitations for celebrity clients, her careful script decorating the envelopes for Robin Thicke and Paula Patton's wedding, her hand creating elegance for people whose names she recognised from magazines. Modelling for briefcase girls on game shows, standing on stage holding prizes, smiling on cue, being decorative.

The game show work was strange. *Deal or No Deal* paid decently and required minimal preparation. Wearing identical evening gowns, 26 women, each holding a briefcase containing a different dollar amount, standing on risers while contestants tried to guess their way to a fortune. The producers wanted energy, enthusiasm, glamour. They wanted women who could smile for hours without the smile ever faltering. Before each taping, they lined the women up for inspection. Padding was added to bras. Stomachs were told to be sucked in. The instruction was explicit. Be beautiful, be decorative, be nothing else.

Meghan could do that. She'd been doing it for years. But standing under those lights, she felt herself reduced to a body holding a box, a smile attached to a number. The other women were smart, interesting, ambitious. Between takes they talked about their real lives, their real goals, the careers they were building when they weren't standing on risers being ornamental. The job paid the bills. It also clarified something. She hadn't trained at Northwestern to be a human prop.

But standing there under the hot stage lights, she'd think about Northwestern, about Vincent, about all those hours learning to build characters brick by brick. She'd think about Sally Bowles falling apart on stage, about the ambassador in Buenos Aires, about international relations and diplomacy and everything she'd studied that had nothing to do with holding a briefcase and looking pretty. This isn't why I learned Shakespeare. The thought would come unbidden, and she'd push it down, fix her smile, gesture at the briefcase as if it contained something that mattered.

Rent was rent. Dignity was a luxury you couldn't always afford when you were 24 and unknown and the alternative was going home to admit you'd failed.

The catering jobs were oddly educational. She'd work parties in Beverly Hills mansions, moving through rooms where deals were being made and careers were being launched, invisible in her black uniform and white apron. She'd hear executives talk about castings, about actors being considered, about the industry's inner workings discussed as if the staff were furniture. They didn't lower their voices when she passed. They didn't even see her.

"You're good at this," another server told her once. "The invisible thing. Most actors hate it."

"I'm watching," Meghan replied. "Learning."

"Learning what?"

"How power moves."

The first real role came in 2006. A brief appearance on *General Hospital*, the soap her father had lit for years. It wasn't nepotism. She'd auditioned like everyone else. But the connection to her father made it feel circular, as if her life were folding back on itself, depositing her in the same studios where she'd watched him work as a child.

The role was small. A nurse with two lines. But it was a union job, which meant benefits, legitimacy, the sense that she was moving forward even if the steps were tiny. Other small parts followed. A few lines on *CSI*. A guest spot on *90210*. Nothing that would launch a career, but enough to keep hope alive.

She met Trevor Engelson at a party in 2004. He was working in the industry as a talent manager and producer, ambitious in ways that matched her own. They dated for years, the relationship easy in some ways, complicated in others. They married in 2011 in Jamaica. A beach wedding, intimate and warm, surrounded by people who loved them.

But the marriage struggled almost immediately. Geography became a problem when Meghan started travelling more for auditions. Ambition became a problem when Trevor expected her to prioritise his career over hers, to be the supportive wife rather than the equal partner they'd promised each other they'd be.

One evening in late 2012, she came home from a shoot, exhausted, carrying scripts for scenes she needed to learn. Trevor was visiting for the weekend, a routine they'd fallen into around each other's jobs. He had news about a project he was producing, wanted her input on casting decisions, needed her to read through notes he'd prepared. She sat at the kitchen table with her own scripts, trying to focus on her lines while he talked through his plans.

Eventually he stopped mid-sentence, looked at her work spread across the table, and said quietly, "You're not even listening." She was listening. She was just also working. But in that moment, she understood something fundamental had broken. He needed a wife who put his work first. She needed a partner who understood hers mattered equally. They couldn't both be right. Someone had to give. And neither of them was willing to be the one who did.

They separated in 2013, divorced shortly after. The split was painful but necessary. She had chosen someone based on who they'd both been at 20-something. They hadn't grown in the same direction. And staying would have meant one of them shrinking to fit the other's expanding life.

Years later, after Meghan's engagement to Harry was announced, Trevor would pitch a television series to Fox. The premise was a man whose wife leaves him when she becomes a princess. The show wasn't picked up, but the pitch made headlines.

In Toronto, she began dating Cory Vitiello, a chef who owned several restaurants in the city. The relationship was easy in ways her marriage hadn't been. He understood irregular schedules, creative ambition, the particular exhaustion of building something from nothing. They were together for nearly two years, part of Toronto's food and social scene, comfortable and stable. When it ended in 2016, the split was quiet, undramatic, just two people who'd enjoyed each other's company but weren't building toward the same future.

Even while hustling through auditions and survival jobs, Meghan maintained her advocacy work. She volunteered with organisations supporting women and girls. She travelled on a clean water initiative to Rwanda, spending a week in rural communities where access to water meant hours of daily labour for women and girls who could be in school, starting businesses, doing anything except walking miles with heavy containers balanced on their heads.

She wrote about the experience, submitted pieces to online platforms. One article got picked up, then another. She wasn't being paid, but she was building a portfolio that wasn't just head-shots and acting clips.

By 2010, Meghan's career had reached a plateau. She was working regularly. Guest spots, recurring roles, nothing permanent but enough to qualify as a working actor. She'd landed an agent, got SAG insurance, could legitimately call herself a professional. But she wasn't a name. Wasn't someone casting directors requested.

She thought about quitting sometimes. Going back to school. Using her IR degree for something stable. The plateau felt sustainable but also suffocating, like she could stay here forever without ever breaking through.

"How long do you give yourself?" a friend asked over dinner one night.

"Give myself?"

"Before you call it. Most actors set a deadline. Five years, ten years. A point where they stop and reassess."

Meghan thought about it. "I don't think I can set one. Because I don't know what else I'd do."

"That's either dedication or delusion."

"Probably both," Meghan agreed.

When her agent called about *Suits* in 2011, Meghan almost didn't take the audition seriously. Another legal drama. Another audition that probably wouldn't lead anywhere. Another day of preparing sides and hoping for a callback that might never come.

But something about the character description caught her attention. Rachel Zane. Paralegal with photographic memory, working towards becoming a lawyer, dealing with test anxiety that kept her from passing the bar. Smart, capable, vulnerable. A woman with her own arc, her own ambitions, her own story that existed independent of the male lead.

She filmed her audition tape in the back room of a friend's restaurant, the only quiet space available on short notice. The lighting was wrong. The background was wrong. But Rachel came through anyway, brick by brick, the way Vincent had taught her.

"This feels different," Meghan told her agent.

"Don't get your hopes up."

Too late. She was already building the character brick by brick.

She prepared for the audition with the thoroughness Vincent had taught her at Northwestern. She studied Rachel's backstory, her fears, her defences. Found the emotional truth beneath the competence. When she walked into the audition room in Toronto, she wasn't performing confidence. She was confident. She knew this woman. She understood her.

The scene was Rachel confronting someone who'd underestimated her. Meghan delivered the lines with quiet fury, with intelligence that didn't need to announce itself, with the dignity of someone who'd spent years proving herself in rooms that doubted her.

When she finished, the silence in the room stretched long enough to become its own thing. The casting director looked at her. The producer looked at her. Nobody spoke for what felt like a full minute.

"Thank you," the casting director said finally. "That was great. We'll be in touch."

She flew back to Los Angeles not daring to hope, but hoping anyway. The next three days felt endless. Every time her phone rang, her heart would stop, and then it would be someone else, something else, not the call she was waiting for.

On day three, her agent called.

"You got it. They're offering you the role."

Meghan sat down on her apartment floor. Her legs simply stopped working, and she was on the ground with the phone still pressed to her ear, looking at the Murphy bed and the dying plants and the head-shots that had gone nowhere for eight years.

"When do they need me in Toronto?" she asked.

"Two weeks. Start packing."

She hung up and called her mother.

"I got it," she said when Doria answered.

"The show?"

"Yeah. The show."

Doria paused, and Meghan heard her take a breath. "I'm so proud of you, baby."

"I haven't done anything yet."

"You did everything. You kept going. That's the hardest part."

After they hung up, Meghan stayed on the floor for a while. The apartment looked the same as it had an hour ago. The same struggling plants, the same Murphy bed, the same kitchen where she'd eaten too many cheap dinners wondering if any of this was ever going to work. But something changed. Eight years of brick by brick, and finally, finally, the structure was starting to hold.

She stood up. Looked around the apartment one last time.

Then she started packing for Toronto.

"Meghan Markle is a ruthless social climbing actress who has landed the role of her life and is determined to milk it for all she can and that's why the Palace is beginning to turn on her"
Piers Morgan, *Daily Mail*, 4 December 2018

3

'Suits Her'

Toronto in August felt like a city holding its breath before autumn. Meghan stepped out of Pearson Airport into air that was warm but carried an edge, a hint of the season turning. She'd packed for what she imagined Canadian weather would be, which turned out to be inadequate. The taxi driver, sensing her confusion about the address, offered gentle navigation tips in an accent she couldn't quite place. She liked him immediately. The city already felt different from Los Angeles. Quieter. Less performed.

The apartment she'd rented sight unseen sat in the Annex, a neighbourhood with tree-lined streets and Victorian houses converted into flats. The estate agent met her with keys and a patient explanation of how the radiators worked, which rubbish went in which bin, where the nearest shops were. Meghan signed papers, accepted the keys, and stood alone in the empty space after the agent left.

Two bedrooms. Hardwood floors. Windows that let in eastern light. A kitchen with white tiles and a gas hob that clicked when you turned it on. She set her suitcase down and walked through each room, running her hand along the walls, looking out each window at views she'd be seeing for years if this worked. If this worked. The "if" still felt enormous. She'd had roles before, small ones, parts that led nowhere. This could be more of the same. Or it could be the thing that changed everything.

She sat on the floor in the empty living room, her back against the wall, and let herself feel the full weight of what she'd done. Quit her survival jobs. Packed up her LA apartment. Moved to a foreign country for a television show that might get cancelled after six episodes. Her savings would last maybe four months if it all fell apart. After that, she didn't know. But she was here. She'd made the choice. Now she had to make it work.

The first day on set came too quickly. She woke at five, nerves humming beneath her skin in a way they hadn't during auditions. Auditions were controlled environments, just her and a few people in a room, stakes high but private. This was different. This was showing up and having to deliver in front of cameras and crew and actors who'd been doing this longer than she had. This was the beginning of something that would either work or publicly fail, and there was no hiding from either outcome.

She dressed carefully. Rachel Zane's wardrobe lived somewhere between power and approachability. Meghan had studied the sides enough to understand the character's psychology, but translating that into physical presence required choices. Hair down. Minimal jewellery. Confidence without aggression.

The production facility sat in an industrial part of the city, all concrete and glass, converted warehouse space that hummed with activity even at six in the morning. Security waved her through. Someone with a headset and clipboard found her immediately, guided her through corridors that smelled like coffee and industrial carpet, delivered her to a trailer with her name on the door.

Her name, on a door.

She stood outside for a moment, just looking at it. A piece of paper, printed and taped at eye level. 'MEGHAN MARKLE'. Eight years of auditions and rejection and waiting tables and holding briefcases, and here was her name on a door. It didn't matter that the trailer was small, that the paper would yellow and curl at the edges, that a hundred actors had used this same trailer before her. Right now, it was hers.

She went inside, sat on the small sofa, and let that reality sink in. The trailer smelled like industrial cleaner and something floral, probably left by whoever had used it last. There was a mirror with lights around it, a rack for costumes, a tiny bathroom. Ordinary. Functional. And completely surreal.

A knock interrupted her thoughts. "Ms Markle? Hair and makeup in five."

The hair and makeup trailer was controlled chaos. Three chairs, three artists working simultaneously on different cast members, music playing low, the particular intimacy that develops amongst people who see each other at five in the morning before coffee has kicked in. A woman with kind eyes and deft hands gestured Meghan into a chair.

"I'm Sarah," she said. "I'll be doing your hair for the show."

"Nice to meet you."

"Excited for your first day?"

"Terrified."

Sarah laughed. "Good. The terrified ones work harder."

Patrick J. Adams walked in halfway through Meghan's makeup application, already in costume, looking exactly like Mike Ross even at this ungodly hour. He caught her eye in the mirror and smiled.

"You must be Rachel."

"Meghan."

"Patrick. But everyone calls me Patrick, so that's easy." He poured himself coffee from an industrial-sized carafe. "First day?"

"Is it that obvious?"

"You're the only one who looks awake. Give it a week."

The table read happened before filming, the full cast assembled in a conference room with scripts and nervous energy and the particular tension that comes when strangers are about to become colleagues. Aaron Korsh, the show-runner, sat at the head of the table, radiating the quiet authority of someone who'd created this world and knew exactly how it should sound.

"Welcome to *Suits*," he said simply. "Let's see what we've got."

Meghan had done table reads before, but never for something this substantial. As they worked through the pilot script, she felt the room's energy shift. The dialogue was sharp. The characters had distinct voices. And Rachel, her Rachel, had scenes that mattered. She wasn't decoration, or the love interest who existed only to further the male lead's arc. She had her own ambitions, her own obstacles, her own intelligence that didn't require dumbing down to make the men look smarter.

When they finished, Aaron looked around the table. "That's what I was hoping for. You all sound like people, not characters. Let's keep that."

Gabriel Macht, who played Harvey Specter, caught Meghan after the read. "You've got good instincts with Rachel. Don't let anyone talk you out of them."

"Thank you."

"I mean it. Sometimes shows want to smooth out the interesting bits. Rachel works because she's got edges. The test anxiety, the perfectionism, the way she's been underestimated her whole life. Those are features, not bugs. Protect them."

The first few weeks of filming blurred together in a rhythm Meghan hadn't experienced since Northwestern. Early calls, long days under lights, endless takes, adjustments, the peculiar boredom of waiting punctuated by bursts of intense focus. But the cast and crew developed a camaraderie that surprised her. Television sets could be toxic, competitive, ruled by egos. This one wasn't. People helped each other. The crew made jokes between takes. Directors treated actors like collaborators rather than puppets.

Somewhere in the third week, something shifted. Meghan was shooting a scene where Rachel confronts a senior partner who's dismissed her ideas. The first few takes were fine, professional, hitting the beats. But something wasn't landing. The director called cut, came over to talk to her.

"It's good," he said. "But I want to try something. This guy has been underestimating Rachel for years. Every time she has a good idea, he takes credit. Every time she proves herself, he moves the goalposts. She's not just frustrated in this scene. She's been carrying this for a long time."

Meghan thought about the auditions where she'd been told she was too ethnic, not clear enough, too much of something or not enough of something else. She thought about the casting directors who'd looked at her headshot and then at her face and couldn't reconcile the two. She thought about every room where she'd had to prove she belonged before anyone would listen to what she had to say.

"Let's go again," she said.

This time, when she delivered Rachel's lines, it all clicked. The words were the same, but the weight behind them was different. Real. When she finished, the director was smiling.

"There it is," he said. "That's what we need."

One evening after a particularly long shoot, Gina Torres invited her for a drink. They went to a quiet bar near the studio, the kind of place that catered to industry people who didn't want to be bothered. Gina ordered scotch. Meghan ordered wine.

"How are you finding it?" Gina asked.

"Finding what?"

"The show. Toronto. All of it."

Meghan considered. "Honestly? It feels like the first time I'm being seen properly."

"Seen as what?"

"As someone who can do the job. Not as someone who has to prove she's not just a pretty face, or justify why she's in the room, or explain what ethnicity she is before anyone will take her seriously."

Gina nodded slowly. "That's what good writing does. It gives you room to be competent without apology."

"I'm trying not to get too attached. If we don't get picked up..."

"We'll get picked up," Gina said with the certainty of someone who'd been doing this long enough to recognise quality. "Aaron knows what he's doing. And the chemistry's there. You can't fake that."

Suits premiered in June 2011 to solid reviews and respectable numbers. Not a phenomenon, not a flop. Just steady, professional television that found its audience and kept them. Meghan's phone started buzzing with messages from people she hadn't heard from in years. Congratulations. I always knew you'd make it. Let's catch up.

She responded politely but recognised the pattern. Success made people reappear.

Toronto settled into rhythms. Filming days that started before dawn and ended after dark. Table reads on Monday mornings. Costume fittings. Script revisions. Exhaustion from saying the same lines twenty times with slightly different inflections until the director finds what they're looking for. But Meghan liked the structure. She rented a house in the Annex, a two-storey Victorian with a small garden and radiators that clanked at night. She furnished it slowly. A sofa from a second-hand shop. Plants she promised herself she'd keep alive this time. Photographs from Northwestern and Los Angeles.

She discovered yoga studios that opened at six. Coffee shops where baristas learnt her order. Running routes along the waterfront where the city stretched out beside Lake Ontario. She made friends outside the industry, people who didn't care that she was on television, who invited her to dinner parties and book clubs and weekend trips to cottages north of the city.

Jessica Mulroney became her closest friend in Toronto, a stylist and television personality who understood the peculiar pressures of being visible. Jessica helped her navigate fashion choices for press events, introduced her to designers, became the person Meghan called when she needed advice about anything from relationships to red carpets.

She'd met Serena Williams years earlier, at a Super Bowl event in 2010, two women in the early stages of careers that would take them in directions neither could have predicted. They'd stayed in touch, the friendship deepening over time, built on mutual respect and the particular understanding that came from being ambitious women in industries that didn't always welcome ambition.

Patrick became her closest friend on set. They had an ease with each other that translated into Mike and Rachel's chemistry but existed independently of it. He was married, grounded, the kind of actor who cared more about craft than celebrity.

One day between takes, they sat on the Pearson Specter set, surrounded by the fake law office that had become more familiar than some real spaces in her life.

"Do you ever feel weird about it?" she asked.

"About what?"

"Playing lawyers. Like we're pretending to be important."

Patrick laughed. "We're actors. Pretending is the job."

"I know, but. Rachel went to law school. She worked for years to pass the bar. We just show up and read words someone else wrote."

"And then millions of people watch and some of them think, maybe I could go to law school. Maybe I could work that hard. Maybe I could be that determined. That's not nothing."

She started *The Tig* in 2014, during the show's third season. The idea had been forming for months, a restlessness that acting alone couldn't satisfy. She loved playing Rachel, but Rachel was someone else's creation. *The Tig* would be hers.

She named it after Tignanello wine, the first really good bottle she'd ever tasted, the one that taught her what people meant when they talked about wine "having a moment." That feeling of encountering something that shifts your understanding, opens a door you didn't know was there. She wanted the blog to do that. Not curated Instagram perfection, but actual writing about travel, food, women she admired, causes that mattered to her.

The blog found an audience accidentally. Women who watched *Suits* wanted to know more about her. But also women who didn't watch television, who just appreciated thoughtful writing about living with intention. She interviewed female politicians, activists, writers. She wrote about menstrual health in developing countries, about education barriers for girls, about water access and how its absence trapped women in poverty.

But coverage of *The Tig* focused on fashion recommendations and travel destinations. Speeches about women's empowerment would later be covered as, "Meghan Wears £2,000 Dress to Charity Event."

Her work with organisations supporting survivors of violence would generate headlines about her hair. She could speak about structural inequality for an hour. The coverage would focus on whether she'd curtseyed correctly. She posted recipes for week-night dinners. She recommended books.

Some people in her professional circle thought it was risky. Giving away so much of yourself for free, building a brand outside your work, making yourself accessible in ways that could backfire.

Meghan didn't see it that way. *The Tig* was her voice when she wasn't playing Rachel. It was the part of her that had written letters to Procter & Gamble at eleven, that had interned at embassies, that cared about the world beyond sound-stages and call sheets.

Sarah Rafferty, who played Donna on the show, understood. They'd become close during the second season, bonding over shared exhaustion and dark humour and the particular cama-raderie of women working in a male-dominated industry.

One evening, after filming a particularly long courtroom scene, they collapsed in Sarah's trailer with tea and biscuits some-one had left in craft services.

"I read your latest *Tig* post," Sarah said. "The one about girls missing school because of periods."

"Did it sound preachy?"

"It sounded like you give a shit. Which is rarer than you'd think."

"I'm trying to figure out how to use whatever visibility I'm getting for things that matter."

"You're already doing it," Sarah said. "Just don't let anyone convince you that caring makes you less professional."

By season four, *Suits* had become something rare in television. Not a phenomenon that burnt bright and fast, but steady, re-spected programming that built audience gradually. Critics praised the writing. Fans obsessed over the characters. Meghan's face started appearing in magazines, usually in those "Who Wore It Best" sections she'd never imagined being part of.

She travelled when the show was on hiatus. Rwanda with World Vision, working on clean water projects. India, Afghanistan.

She took notebooks, not cameras. She talked to women about their lives, their barriers, their hopes. She wrote about it, sometimes for *The Tig*, sometimes for platforms that paid her in exposure rather than money.

One trip to India, she spent a week in rural communities talking to adolescent girls about menstruation stigma. The shame that kept them home from school, the taboos that made normal biology feel like curse. She listened more than she spoke. She asked questions. She tried to understand systems she'd never had to navigate.

A teenage girl asked her, through a translator, why she cared.

"Because when you know better, you do better," Meghan said. It was Oprah's line, but she meant it.

The girl smiled. "You came a long way to tell us we matter."

"You do matter. And your education matters. And you shouldn't have to miss school because of something completely natural."

The UN Women speech came in 2015. They invited her to speak about gender equality at their New York headquarters. She said yes before fully processing what that meant. Public speaking terrified her in ways auditions never had. Auditions, you could retry. Speeches happened once, in front of people who would judge every word.

The night before, she barely slept. She lay in her hotel room running through the speech in her head, imagining everything that could go wrong. Forgetting her lines. Stumbling over words. The audience realising she was just an actress, not a real advocate, not someone who deserved to be speaking at the United Nations.

Patrick helped her practice in her trailer between takes in the weeks leading up to it.

"You're over-thinking it," he said, after she'd stumbled through the opening for the fourth time.

"I'm speaking at the UN."

"You're talking about something you've been working on for years. Just talk like you're talking to me."

The morning of the speech, she stood backstage, hands shaking. The room was full of diplomats, activists, journalists. Real people doing real work. And here she was, a woman who pretended to be a lawyer on television, about to tell them about gender equality.

Then she thought about the girl in India. You came a long way to tell us we matter. She thought about all the letters she'd received from young women who'd read *The Tig* and felt seen. She thought about her mother calling the school about the form, about the box that hadn't existed until someone insisted it should.

She walked to the podium.

The speech went well. She spoke about women's economic participation, about structural barriers, about the need for systemic change. She told the story of the Procter & Gamble letter, how an eleven-year-old had changed the wording of a commercial by speaking up. She talked about the power of voice, of refusing to accept things as they were simply because that's how they'd always been.

She didn't become viral-famous, but the speech got coverage, respectful coverage from outlets that mattered. And girls started writing to her, sharing their own stories, asking for advice.

Her mother called after watching a video of the speech.

"I'm proud of you, baby."

"I was so nervous I thought I'd throw up."

"You didn't look nervous. You looked like someone who knew what she was talking about."

"I'm still just an actor on a cable show."

"You're a woman using her voice. Don't diminish that."

By 2016, Meghan's life had found equilibrium. *Suits* was renewed for a seventh season. *The Tig* had become a small business, bringing in modest income from partnerships and sponsored content. She'd bought a house in Toronto properly, not just rented. Put down roots in a city that had given her privacy, stability, respect.

Cory was part of that Toronto life by then. They went to restaurants where he knew the owners. They cooked together in his kitchen. They existed in a comfortable present tense without discussing what came next.

One evening in July, she was cooking dinner in her kitchen when her phone buzzed with a text from a friend in London. Someone she trusted, someone who didn't traffic in gossip or drama.

"I have someone I want you to meet. I think you two would really hit it off."

Meghan replied with casual interest. Her life was full. Her work was consuming. But the friend was persistent in the gentlest way. And something in that persistence made Meghan curious.

"Tell me more," she texted back.

The response came quickly. "Let's talk properly. Can I call you?"

Meghan set down her wooden spoon, turned off the hob.

"Sure," she typed. "Call me now."

She picked up on the second ring.

"Tell me about him," she said.

"If there is issue from Meghan Markle's alleged union
with Prince Harry, the Windsors will thicken their watery,
thin blue blood and Spencer pale skin and ginger hair
with some rich and exotic DNA"
Rachel Johnson, *Mail on Sunday*, 6 November 2016

4

'Harry's Girl'

The text arrived on a Tuesday evening while Meghan was cooking pasta, her phone buzzing against the kitchen counter beside a half-empty glass of wine. She glanced at it, expecting a message from her agent or a friend confirming weekend plans. Instead, she read the name of someone she trusted completely, followed by words that made her pause mid-stir.

"I know someone you should meet."

Meghan set down the wooden spoon. The sauce bubbled quietly. Through the window, Toronto's summer light was starting to soften, the sky turning that particular shade of pale gold that made the city feel almost European. She picked up her phone and read the message again. Her friend wasn't prone to matchmaking. This wasn't the sort of casual suggestion people toss out at dinner parties. There was weight in the phrasing, a deliberate care.

She typed back. "Who?"

The reply came quickly. "Can't say yet. But I think you'd really like him. He's in London next week. Are you around?"

Meghan leaned against the counter. London. She was meant to be there anyway for a charity event and a few meetings.

The timing felt convenient, almost suspiciously so. She'd grown cautious about blind dates over the years. They always seemed to carry the faint air of desperation, two people trying too hard to make conversation while mentally composing their exit strategies.

But this felt different. Her friend knew her well enough to understand what mattered, what didn't, what made someone worth meeting beyond surface credentials. And there was something in the secrecy that intrigued her. Who couldn't be named in a text message?

"I'll be there next week," she typed. "Tell me when and where."

The response was immediate.

"I'll set it up. You won't regret this."

Meghan pocketed her phone and returned to the stove, turning down the heat. The pasta water had begun to boil over slightly, hissing as it hit the burner. She stirred the sauce again, watching it thicken, wondering what she'd just agreed to.

London in July carried a warmth that felt borrowed from somewhere else, as if the city were briefly pretending to be Mediterranean. Meghan arrived on a Thursday, her schedule packed with the sort of commitments that made jet lag irrelevant. A meeting about a potential collaboration. Lunch with a friend from university. An evening reception for a women's organisation she'd supported for years. Between those obligations, she found pockets of time to simply walk, to move through streets where no one recognised her.

The meeting was scheduled for Saturday evening at Dean Street Townhouse, a private member's club in Soho. The matchmaker was Violet von Westenholz, whose father had been close to Prince Charles for years. Some accounts would later credit Misha Nonoo, the fashion designer, but the introduction came through Violet, who'd known Harry since childhood and sensed something in Meghan that might fit. Her friend had been deliberately vague about logistics, offering only an address and a time. Meghan appreciated the discretion even as it heightened her nerves. She dressed carefully that afternoon, choosing something elegant but not overdone. A simple dress, a little jewellery, her hair loose. She wanted to look like herself.

The cab dropped her outside a narrow brick building tucked between a bookshop and a wine bar. She checked the address twice before pushing open the unmarked door. Inside, the space felt deliberately understated. Low lighting, soft music, the kind of atmosphere designed to make conversation feel private even in a crowded room. A woman at the desk greeted her with a smile that suggested she'd been expecting someone but wasn't entirely sure who. "I'm meeting a friend," Meghan said. "I think they've already arrived."

The woman nodded toward a corner where the lighting was dimmer still. "Through there. They're waiting."

Meghan walked slowly, her heels quiet against the wooden floor. The room opened into a smaller space, more intimate, with leather sofas arranged around low tables. Her friend stood near the far wall, drink in hand, smiling in that particular way people smile when they believe they're about to witness something significant. And beside her, turning slightly as Meghan approached, was a man she didn't recognise immediately.

He was tall, casually dressed in a way that suggested he hadn't over-thought the evening. His posture carried a faint tension. Their eyes met. He smiled, a small, tentative thing that softened his face. Meghan felt her own smile arrive instinctively, surprised by how easy it was.

"Meghan," her friend said, stepping forward. "This is Harry."

The name registered a beat later than it should have, the way familiar words sometimes take a moment to connect to their meaning.

Harry. Not just Harry. That Harry. She felt her breath catch briefly, then steady. Her mind was racing through implications, through questions, through everything this meant if it was actually what it seemed to be. But her face stayed calm. Years of auditions had taught her that much.

He extended his hand.

"Hi," he said. His voice was quieter than she expected, a little uncertain. "Thanks for coming. I know this is a bit unusual."

She took his hand. His grip was firm but not performative. "Hi," she replied. "I'm not sure what usual looks like anymore."

He laughed. A real laugh, quick and genuine, and she felt joy at the sound of it. Their friend excused herself with the subtlety of someone who knew exactly when to disappear, murmuring something about needing to check her phone. Meghan and Harry were left standing in the dim corner of a London club, two people who had arrived with vastly different expectations and were now trying to find their footing.

"Should we sit?" he asked, gesturing toward one of the sofas.

"Please," she said. "My feet are already regretting these shoes."

They sat, the space between them polite but not rigid. A server appeared, took their drink orders, and vanished. The silence that followed wasn't uncomfortable, just careful. Meghan studied him in the low light. He looked tired in a way that felt familiar, the tiredness of someone who spent a lot of energy managing how they were perceived. His eyes held a watchful, cautious warmth.

She realised she was looking for the tabloid version of him, the one she'd seen in passing on magazine covers. The party prince. The rebel royal. But the man sitting across from her didn't match that image. He seemed quieter. More guarded. More real.

"So," he said after a moment. "I should probably apologise in advance if this is wildly awkward."

"It's not," she said. "Not yet, anyway."

He smiled again, more relaxed this time. "Good. That's a start."

Their drinks arrived. Meghan sipped her wine, grateful for something to do with her hands. Harry lifted his beer, paused, then set it down without drinking. He looked at her with an expression that was part curiosity, part relief.

"I wasn't sure you'd come," he said. "I wasn't even sure I should ask."

"Why not?"

"Because this is strange. All of it. The setup, the circumstances, the fact that I'm sitting here trying not to sound like an idiot."

Meghan laughed. "You're doing fine. Better than fine, actually."

"I don't usually do this," he continued. "Blind dates. Setups. Any of it. But our friend was very insistent."

"She was insistent with me too," Meghan said. "I think she enjoys orchestrating things."

"She does." He picked up his beer again, this time taking a drink. "So, what do you actually know about me? I mean, aside from the obvious."

Meghan considered the question. The truth was, she knew less than most people would assume. She'd lived in Toronto for years, absorbed in work that didn't require following British tabloids. She knew he was a prince, obviously. She knew his mother had died young and tragically. She knew there had been headlines about him over the years, some sympathetic, some less so. But the details felt distant, like stories about someone she'd never meet.

"Not much," she admitted. "I know you're not just a tabloid headline. I know you've done work with veterans and mental health. Beyond that, I'm coming in fairly blank."

He sighed, and relaxed a little. "That's actually the best answer you could have given."

"Why?"

"Because most people think they know me before I open my mouth. It's exhausting."

She understood that more than he probably realised. "I get that," she said quietly. "Different context, but I get it."

He looked at her with a sharpness that felt like recognition. "You're an actress, right? *Suits*?"

"I am. Seven years now."

"Do people do that to you? Decide who you are before you've said anything?"

"Sometimes. Not as intensely as they might with you, but yes. It's strange, being recognised for playing someone who isn't you."

"Strange is a... generous word for it," he said. "I'd use something stronger, but we've only just met."

Meghan smiled. She liked the way he spoke, the way humour slipped in without forcing its way to the surface. She liked the tiredness in his eyes because it felt honest. She liked that he seemed genuinely curious about her rather than trying to impress her with stories or credentials.

The conversation found its rhythm quickly after that. They talked about travel, about cities they'd loved and cities they'd endured. About work that felt meaningful and work that felt like obligation.

Harry described a recent trip to Africa, his voice becoming more animated, more alive. Meghan told him about her advocacy work, about the communities she'd visited and the women she'd met. Neither of them performed. They simply talked.

At some point, their friend reappeared, checked that they were still breathing, and disappeared again. Time moved strangely in that dim room. An hour felt like ten minutes. Meghan found herself leaning forward, elbows on her knees, the formality of the evening dissolving into something more natural.

Harry had softened too. He was no longer holding himself like someone braced for scrutiny. He was just sitting, talking, laughing at something she'd said about the absurdities of auditions.

"Do you ever feel like you're performing even when you're not working?" she asked at one point. "Like the world expects a version of you that isn't quite real?"

Harry set down his drink and looked at her with an expression that was suddenly very serious.

"Every day," he said. "Every single day."

"It gets tiring," she said.

"It does."

They sat in that acknowledgment for a short while, the noise of the club around them fading into background texture. The conversation had moved from getting-to-know-you pleasantries into something more honest. They were talking about things she didn't usually discuss with people she'd just met.

The evening stretched on. They ordered food without thinking, picking at plates of small things neither of them remembered later. Harry talked about his work with wounded veterans, the way their resilience humbled him. Meghan talked about the disconnect between acting and advocacy, the way people sometimes dismissed the latter because of the former. He asked thoughtful questions. She answered honestly. He listened without interrupting. She did the same.

When they finally stood to leave, the club had emptied around them without either noticing. Their friend had long since gone home, messaging Meghan to say she trusted they'd find their own way out. Harry walked Meghan to the door, the summer air outside still warm despite the late hour. London hummed around them, traffic and distant voices and the particular energy of a city that never quite sleeps. They stood on the pavement, neither quite ready to say goodbye. Meghan tucked her hair behind her ear. Harry shoved his hands in his pockets, looking at her with reluctance to let the evening end.

"Can I see you again?" he asked. "I mean, before you go back to Toronto?"

"I'd like that," she said. The answer came without hesitation.

"Tomorrow? Or is that too soon?"

She smiled. "Tomorrow works for me."

They exchanged numbers. He hugged her briefly, a quick, warm gesture that felt natural rather than calculated. Then he stepped back, already pulling out his phone to call a car. Meghan walked to the corner to hail a cab, glancing back once to see him still standing there, watching her go.

In the taxi, she leaned her head against the cool window and closed her eyes. The evening replayed in fragments. His laugh. The way he'd listened. The tiredness in his eyes that matched something in her own. She didn't know what would come next. She didn't know if tomorrow would feel as easy as tonight. She just knew she wanted to find out.

Her phone buzzed. A text from Harry. "Made it to my car. Thanks for tonight. I'm really glad you came."

She typed back. "Me too."

She didn't sleep much that night. Not from anxiety, but from a restless energy that kept her mind turning. She replayed their conversation, searching for missteps and finding none. She thought about the way he'd looked at her when she'd spoken about her work, the genuine interest in his expression. She thought about his hands, the way they'd moved when he talked, animated and unselfconscious. She thought about his voice, the way it softened when he spoke about things that mattered to him.

And she thought about what it meant. Who he was. What his life actually looked like from the inside. She'd seen enough tabloid coverage over the years to know the public version, the one built from paparazzi photos and anonymous sources. But the man she'd met tonight didn't match that version. He was quieter. More searching. More wounded, maybe.

She thought about his mother. About the photographs she'd seen as a child, Princess Diana in her elegance and sadness, hunted by cameras until the very end. She thought about what it must have been like to grow up in the aftermath of that, to be twelve years old and walking behind a coffin while the whole world watched.

By morning, she'd convinced herself she was over-thinking everything. It had been one evening. One conversation. She dressed for their second meeting with the same care as the first, trying to look effortless while feeling anything but. He'd suggested a walk, somewhere quiet, away from the noise of central London. She agreed, grateful for the simplicity of the plan.

Their third date was Botswana. The suggestion had been Harry's, spontaneous and slightly mad, the kind of thing you only proposed when you were falling fast and didn't want to slow down. He'd been going to the country since childhood, knew it as a place where he could breathe, where the person he was mattered less than the landscape he was in. He wanted to share it with her. She said yes without hesitation, the kind of yes that signals something significant, the willingness to disappear into the African bush with someone you've known for weeks.

They camped under stars, cooked over fires, existed without staff or schedules or the particular pressure of being watched. Meghan saw a different Harry there, looser, lighter, unburdened by the weight he carried at home. He talked about his mother, about losing her, about the ways that loss had shaped everything that came after. She talked about her own complications, her father, the divorce, the identity questions she'd navigated her whole life. They were building something in that wilderness, laying foundations in a place where neither of them was performing.

When they returned to London, the relationship had accelerated past the point of casual. They were serious now, both of them, even if the world didn't know yet.

They met in a park, the sort of wide green space that felt improbable in a city so dense. Harry arrived first, wearing sunglasses and a baseball cap that made him look more conspicuous rather than less. She laughed when she saw him.

"Incognito?" she asked.

"Attempting it," he said, smiling. "Not sure it's working."

They walked slowly, the path winding between trees that offered patches of shade against the afternoon heat. For a while, they said nothing, the silence comfortable rather than strained. Meghan watched the way sunlight filtered through the leaves, casting shifting patterns on the ground.

"I didn't sleep much last night," he said eventually. "Kept thinking about our conversation."

"Same," she admitted. "I kept wondering if I'd said something stupid."

"You didn't. You were honest. That's rare."

"So were you."

He glanced at her, his expression unreadable behind the sunglasses. "I want to be honest with you about something."

"Okay."

"This is complicated. My life, I mean. The logistics of it. The scrutiny. The way the press operates. I don't want to scare you off, but I also don't want to pretend it's simple."

Meghan stopped walking. He stopped too, turning to face her. She could see herself reflected in his sunglasses, small and slightly distorted. She thought about his mother, about the photographers who'd chased Diana through a Paris tunnel. About the girlfriends who'd appeared briefly beside him and then vanished, driven away by the attention or the pressure or both.

"I appreciate the honesty," she said carefully. "But I'm not someone who scares easily."

"I know. I can tell. But there's knowing in theory and knowing in practice. The press can be brutal. Especially to people close to me."

"I understand what you're saying," she said. "And I'm not going into this blind. But I also think we're getting ahead of ourselves. This is only our second meeting."

He smiled, some of the tension leaving his shoulders. "You're right. I'm catastrophising."

"A little."

"Occupational hazard."

They resumed walking, the conversation shifting to lighter ground. He asked about her childhood, about growing up in Los Angeles, about the moment she decided she wanted to act. She asked about his work with charities, about the causes that mattered most to him, about the parts of his life that felt most authentic.

The hours passed without either of them noticing.

At some point, they stopped at a bench overlooking a pond. Ducks moved across the surface in lazy arcs, unbothered by the world beyond the water. Harry took off his sunglasses, tucking them into his shirt. His eyes looked lighter in the sun, the green more pronounced.

"Can I ask you something?" he said.

"Of course."

"What do you want? Like, in life. In the big picture."

The question surprised her with its directness. She thought about it, watching the ducks glide across the pond. "I want to do work that matters," she said finally. "I want to use whatever platform I have to help people who don't have one. I want to wake up feeling like I'm contributing something beyond myself."

"And acting? Does that fit into that?"

"Sometimes. When the role is right, when the story says something worth saying. But acting is also just what I do. It's not all of who I am."

He nodded slowly. "I understand that. People think my life is my title. But the title is just a frame. The actual life is everything inside it."

"Exactly."

They sat in the quiet for a while, the afternoon light beginning to shift toward evening. Meghan glanced at him, saw the way he was watching the water, his expression unguarded for once. She wondered what he saw when he looked at her. Whether he was calculating risks the way she was. Whether he felt the same pull she did, the sense that something was happening here that neither of them had quite planned for.

"I should probably head back soon," she said eventually. "I have a dinner thing tonight."

"Can I see you again before you leave?" he asked. "Or is three times in four days too much?"

She laughed. "Three times feels about right."

They stood, stretching slightly after sitting so long. He looked at her with an expression that was suddenly very direct, very present. "I'm really glad I met you," he said. "I don't say that lightly."

"Neither do I. But I'm glad too."

He walked her back through the park, the path more crowded now with families and joggers and couples holding hands. At the edge of the park, where the city reasserted itself in concrete and traffic, they said goodbye again. Another brief hug, his hand lingering on her arm for just a second longer than necessary.

The third time they met, the ease had solidified into something unmistakable. They had dinner at a small restaurant chosen for its discretion, tucked into a basement with dim lighting and tables spaced far enough apart that conversations stayed private.

They talked for hours, the food growing cold on their plates, the restaurant emptying around them. At one point, Harry reached across the table and held her hand.

"I need to tell you something," he said.

She felt her heart quicken. "Okay."

"I'm falling for you. I know it's fast. I know it's complicated. But I can't pretend I'm not."

She looked at their hands, his fingers wrapped around hers. Three meetings. Less than a week. It was fast. It was reckless. It was the kind of thing she'd have counselled any friend against.

"I'm falling for you too," she said quietly. "And it terrifies me."

"Why?"

"Because I can see how hard this could be. The scrutiny, the pressure, the way your world operates. I'm not naive about any of it."

"I know you're not. But I also think we'd figure it out, together."

She looked up at him, saw the vulnerability in his expression, the hope mixed with fear. She thought about walking away, about protecting herself from the storm she could already feel gathering on the horizon. She thought about the life she'd built in Toronto, the equilibrium she'd found, the peace of being known for her work rather than her relationships.

But she also thought about the way he listened, the way he made her laugh, the way his presence felt like something she'd been missing without knowing it. She thought about the loneliness in his eyes that matched something in her own. Two people who knew what it felt like to be seen without being known.

"Okay," she said. "Let's figure it out."

He smiled, relief flooding his face. "Yeah?"

"Yeah."

They left the restaurant late, walking through streets that had emptied into the particular silence of a city after midnight.

Harry held her hand as they walked. They didn't talk much. They didn't need to.

When they reached her hotel, they stood outside for a long moment, neither wanting the evening to end. The night air was cool, carrying the faint smell of rain that hadn't yet fallen. Harry cupped her face in his hands, his expression serious.

"I'm going to do everything I can to protect you," he said. "From all of it. The press, the scrutiny, everything."

She believed him. She could see the conviction in his eyes, the determination. But she also understood something he maybe didn't yet. That protection has limits. That good intentions collide with realities that don't care about love or sincerity.

"Just don't disappear on me," she said. "Whatever happens, don't disappear."

"I won't. I promise."

He kissed her then, soft and careful. When they pulled apart, she felt the shift complete. The life she'd been living had ended. The life ahead had begun. She didn't know yet what that would mean, what it would cost, what it would require her to become.

She just knew she'd chosen it. Chosen him.

Two people, a quiet street, a moment of possibility. And the belief, fragile but real, that love might be enough.

“Buckingham Palace to investigate
claims Meghan bullied staff”
BBC News, 3 March 2021

5

'Duchess Difficult'

The first time Meghan walked through the gates of Kensington Palace, she noticed the silence. There were cars in the distance, voices somewhere beyond the walls, but a particular kind of hush that felt deliberate. The air inside the grounds carried a weight, as if centuries of protocol had pressed themselves into the atmosphere. She followed Harry along a gravel path, her heels making small crunching sounds that seemed too loud, too intrusive. He walked with the ease of someone who had spent his entire life in these spaces, who knew which doors opened with a push and which required a key he kept in his pocket.

"It's quieter than I expected," she said.

He glanced at her, smiled slightly. "It's always quiet. That's part of the design."

She thought about what that meant. Quiet by design. A place built to keep the world out, or perhaps to keep the people inside contained. She couldn't tell yet which it was.

They reached a small cottage tucked behind a larger building, modest by the standards of everything around it.

Two bedrooms, a kitchen, low ceilings that made the space feel almost cosy despite its location. Harry unlocked the door and stepped aside to let her in first. The rooms smelled faintly of old wood and something floral she couldn't quite place. Sunlight came through the windows at an angle, catching dust motes in the air.

"This is Nottingham Cottage," he said. "Nott Cott, if you're feeling informal. It's where I've been living."

Meghan walked slowly through the space, taking in the worn furniture, the books stacked on shelves, the photographs in frames that showed Harry at various ages, always smiling, always surrounded by people. She stopped at the kitchen window, looking out at the perfectly maintained garden beyond. Everything here felt tended, curated, preserved. Nothing felt accidental. She wondered what it was like to grow up in spaces where every blade of grass was monitored, where nothing was allowed to grow wild.

"It's lovely," she said, and she meant it. The cottage had a warmth that surprised her, a sense of being tucked away from the world. She could imagine mornings here, coffee in the quiet, evenings reading by lamplight. But she could also feel the palace beyond these walls, the institution pressing in from all sides.

Harry came up behind her, his hands settling on her shoulders. "I know it's a lot," he said quietly. "The whole thing. The family, the protocols, the way everything works. Or doesn't work, depending on the day."

She turned to face him. "I'm not afraid of complicated," she said.

"I know. But this is a specific kind of complicated."

"Then help me understand it."

He exhaled, then cuddled her. "I'm trying. I promise I'm trying."

The palace sent someone to brief her a week later. A woman named Sarah, polite and efficient, who arrived at Nott Cott with a leather folder and the kind of smile that never quite reached the eyes.

They sat in the small living room, tea cooling on the table between them, while Sarah outlined what would be expected if Meghan's relationship with Harry continued to develop in the direction it seemed to be heading.

"There are protocols," Sarah said, her voice measured. "Ways of doing things that have been established over centuries. They exist for good reason, to maintain consistency, to project the right image to the public."

Meghan nodded, pen in hand, taking notes the way she always did when trying to learn something new. "I understand. What kind of protocols specifically?"

Sarah opened the folder, pulled out a document. "Public appearances, for one. There's a particular way to stand, to walk, to engage with crowds. Eye contact is important but not prolonged. Smiles are warm but not overly familiar. You'll be representing the institution, not just yourself."

"Right," Meghan said. She wrote that down, then looked up. "And what about the work I'm already doing? The advocacy, the charity partnerships?"

Sarah's expression shifted slightly, something careful sliding into place. "That would need to be reviewed. Anything you do publicly reflects on the family, so it would need to align with existing priorities. There are channels for these things, approval processes."

"Approval from who?"

"From the appropriate offices. It's not meant to be restrictive, just protective. The monarchy has to be careful about political associations, about anything that could be seen as taking sides."

Meghan absorbed this. She had spent years building relationships with organisations, had travelled to communities, had written and spoken and showed up. The idea of routing all of that through layers of approval felt suffocating.

But she kept her face neutral, tried to approach it the way she approached everything, with openness and a willingness to adapt.

"What about social media?" she asked. "I have a blog, *The Tig*. It's mostly lifestyle content, travel, recipes, that sort of thing."

Sarah's pause told her the answer before the words came. "That would need to close. Members of the family don't maintain personal social media in that way. It creates vulnerabilities, opens doors that are better left closed."

Meghan set down her pen. "Close it entirely?"

"I'm afraid so. It's standard practice."

The conversation continued for another hour, covering everything from clothing choices to handshakes to the proper way to exit a car without showing too much leg. By the time Sarah left, Meghan felt as though she'd been given a manual for a life she hadn't yet agreed to live. She sat alone in the cottage, staring at the notes she'd taken, trying to square the rules with the person she'd always been. Independent. Outspoken. Unwilling to shrink herself to fit someone else's frame.

Harry came home to find her on the sofa, still holding the notebook. He sat beside her without speaking, just close enough that their shoulders touched. She leaned into him.

"She told you about social media," he said. It wasn't a question.

"She did."

"I'm sorry. I know *The Tig* matters to you."

"It does. It did." She closed the notebook, set it on the table. "But I understand why it has to go. I just wish someone had explained all of this sooner. I feel like I'm learning the rules of a game after I've already started playing."

He took her hand, threaded his fingers through hers. "That's how it works here. They don't explain everything up front because they assume you'll absorb it as you go. Osmosis instead of instruction."

"That's not how I learn."

"I know." He kissed the side of her head. "But you're doing fine. Better than fine. You just have to trust that it gets easier."

She nodded but wasn't completely convinced.

One member of the briefing staff, a woman named Claire who worked in communications, caught Meghan after a subsequent meeting about press protocols. She was perhaps ten years older, efficient but with something warmer underneath the professional manner. She handed Meghan a folder of sample schedules and talking points, then paused.

"If you have questions," Claire said quietly, "you can email me directly. Not through official channels. Just me. The learning curve here is steep, and the institution doesn't always remember that people are learning curves, not just positions to fill."

Meghan looked at her, surprised by the directness. "Thank you."

"Don't thank me yet. I may not be able to fix anything. But I can explain why things work the way they do. Sometimes that helps."

It did help, in small ways. Over the following months, Claire would send occasional emails answering questions Meghan hadn't known how to ask officially. Nothing subversive, just context. History. The reasoning behind protocols that seemed arbitrary. The emails stopped eventually, when Claire was moved to a different department. Meghan never knew if the move was coincidental or consequence.

Meeting the Queen happened on a Sunday afternoon in October 2016, several weeks before the engagement would be announced. Harry drove them to Windsor, the autumn light soft through the windows, leaves turning gold and red along the roads. Meghan dressed carefully, choosing something elegant but not ostentatious, her hair pulled back, minimal jewellery. Her nerves settled.

"Relax," Harry said, glancing at her. "She's going to love you."

"You don't know that."

"I do. She values sincerity. Just be yourself."

They were ushered into a drawing room, the sort of space that felt designed to make people feel simultaneously welcomed and insignificant. High ceilings, oil paintings, furniture that had probably been sitting in the same positions for decades. Meghan stood near the window, hands clasped in front of her, trying to calm her breathing. Then the door opened, and the Queen walked in.

She was smaller than Meghan expected, her presence somehow larger than her physical frame. She moved with a steadiness that came from a lifetime of being watched, assessed, photographed. Her eyes were sharp, taking in everything without seeming to stare. She extended her hand, and Meghan took it, offering a small curtsy the way Harry had taught her.

"Your Majesty," Meghan said. "It's an honour to meet you."

The Queen's smile was warm, genuine. "Harry has told me a great deal about you. Please, sit."

They settled into chairs arranged near the fireplace, tea brought in by staff who moved with practised silence. The Queen poured, her movements precise, unhurried. She asked Meghan about her work, about *Suits*, about the causes she cared about. Meghan answered carefully, aware that every word was being measured, but also trying to be honest, to show the person she actually was rather than a performance of what she thought was expected.

"Harry tells me you're passionate about gender equality," the Queen said, stirring her tea.

"I am," Meghan replied. "I think women everywhere deserve the same opportunities, the same respect. I've been fortunate to work with organisations that focus on education and empowerment."

The Queen nodded. "Admirable. The monarchy has always valued service, though we must be careful about how we engage with political matters. Advocacy can be valuable, but it requires discretion."

"I understand," Meghan said, though she wasn't entirely sure she did. The line between advocacy and politics felt blurry, subjective, something that could shift depending on who was drawing it.

Harry sat beside her, his posture relaxed, but attention focused.

The Queen turned her gaze to Harry. "You seem happy."

He smiled. "I am."

"Good. Happiness is important. But so is duty. The two must coexist."

"They will," he said. "They do."

The Queen's expression softened slightly. "I hope so. For both your sakes."

The visit lasted an hour, polite and pleasant, with no dramatic declarations or profound revelations.

As they drove away, Meghan felt the reality of what had just happened. She had been assessed, evaluated, measured against standards she couldn't entirely see.

"That went well," Harry said as they merged onto the motorway.

"Did it?"

"She liked you. I could tell."

"How?"

"She smiled. She doesn't smile at everyone."

Meghan looked out the window, watching the countryside blur past. She wanted to feel relief. But she couldn't shake the sense that approval was conditional, something to be earned continuously rather than given once.

In the weeks before the press discovered her, Meghan attended a private lunch for one of Harry's patronages, an organisation supporting young people with HIV. No cameras, no announcement. Just a room of teenagers and 20-somethings who'd grown up with the virus, who'd learnt to navigate medical appointments and disclosure decisions and the particular loneliness of carrying a diagnosis that still carried stigma.

Meghan sat beside a young woman named Aisha, perhaps nineteen, who'd been born with HIV and had never told anyone outside her family until joining this organisation. They talked about school, about Aisha's plans to study nursing, about the moment she'd finally told a friend and discovered that friendship could survive honesty.

"Were you scared?" Meghan asked. "When you told her?"

"Terrified. And tired of hiding. Hiding takes so much energy."

Meghan thought about her own life, about the parts she'd learnt to hide depending on context. Not the same as Aisha's experience, but the exhaustion of performing one version of yourself while another version stayed concealed, that she understood.

"It really does," she said.

After the lunch, Harry found her standing by a window, looking at the garden below. "You're good at this," he said.

"At what?"

"Connecting with people. Really connecting, not just going through the motions."

"I like people. I like hearing their stories."

"That's exactly what I mean. Most people in these situations are listening to respond. You're listening to understand."

She turned to face him. "Isn't that the point? Using whatever platform you have to make people feel seen?"

He kissed her forehead. "It should be. It isn't always."

The conversation stayed with her. Whatever else the institution required, she could still do this. Show up. Listen. Remember that the people she met had lives beyond their interaction with her, that her role was to witness rather than to perform witnessing.

The press found out about her in stages. First the whispers, then the speculation, then the full-blown frenzy. Meghan woke one morning to find her name trending on social media, articles dissecting her family, her career, her past relationships. Photographers appeared outside her Toronto apartment, camped on the pavement, waiting for a glimpse of her leaving for work or returning home. She tried going out the back entrance. They found that too. She tried varying her schedule. They adapted. Every time she stepped outside, the clicking started. The shouting of her name. The persistence of people who didn't see her as a person, just content.

Friends warned her not to read the comments, but she did anyway, scrolling through threads late at night when she couldn't sleep. Opportunistic. Calculating. Too ambitious. Not British enough. Too American. Too black. Not black enough. The words accumulated, each one a small cut that healed before the next one landed, so she never quite bled out but never quite stopped hurting either.

Harry called her late one night, his voice tight with frustration. "I've seen the coverage. It's vile."

She was sitting on her bed, laptop open, another article loaded on the screen. This one had dug up her father's bankruptcy filing from years ago, presenting it as evidence of instability, of unsuitability. As if her father's financial struggles were her character flaw. As if poverty were a moral failing she'd inherited.

"It's relentless," she said. "I knew there would be attention, but this feels different. It feels personal."

"It is personal. They're trying to build a narrative before you have a chance to define yourself."

"So what do I do?"

"You ignore it. You do not engage. That is what we have always done."

She heard the exhaustion in his voice, the weariness of someone who had spent his entire life being written about, lied about, reduced to headlines.

"I'm not sure I can do that," she said quietly.

"You have to. If you respond, it escalates. They'll twist anything you say into something worse."

"So I just let them say whatever they want?"

"For now, yes. Until we have a strategy."

She didn't respond. She sat in the dark of her Toronto bedroom, thousands of miles from him, feeling the distance like a physical ache.

The breaking point came in November 2016.

An article appeared in one of the tabloids, framing Meghan's mother in language that was unmistakably coded. Describing her neighbourhood as "dangerous." Her background as "questionable." The article included a photograph of Doria's street, as if to say, look where she comes from. Look what she is.

Meghan read it in a cab on the way to the *Suits* set, her tears blurring the words. She read it twice, trying to find another interpretation, trying to convince herself she was overreacting. But the words were clear. Her mother, the woman who had raised her, who had taught her to speak up, who had called the school about the form, was being reduced to a stereotype. A caricature built from racial assumptions so deeply embedded they didn't even need to be stated explicitly.

By the time she arrived at the studio, she could barely speak. A cast-mate found her in her trailer, asked if she was okay. She shook her head, unable to form words, everything pressing down until it felt like the walls were closing in.

The headlines had a pattern. "Harry's girl is (almost) straight outta Compton," the *Mail* wrote, as if her mother's neighbourhood was an accusation, as if geography determined character.

They called Doria's area "gang-scarred," described it as "crime-ridden," used language that communicated exactly what they meant without quite saying it explicitly. Other papers picked up the framing. Her background was "exotic." Her family was "troubled." She was "different from Harry's usual type" in ways that required no elaboration.

Harry flew to Toronto the next day. He walked into her apartment, took one look at her face, and pulled her into his arms without saying anything. They stood like that for a long time, her face pressed against his chest, his hand moving slowly through her hair.

"I can't do this," she whispered. "I can't keep reading these things and pretending they don't hurt."

"Then don't read them."

"It's not that simple. They're not just attacking me. They're attacking my mother, my family, everything I come from."

He pulled back, looked at her with an intensity that felt almost fierce. "Then I'll make a statement. I'll tell them to stop."

"The palace won't let you."

"I don't care what the palace says. This is my decision."

The statement, when it came, was unprecedented. "His girlfriend, Meghan Markle, has been subject to a wave of abuse and harassment," it read. "Some of this has been very public - the smear on the front page of a national newspaper; the racial undertones of comment pieces; and the outright sexism and racism of social media trolls and web article comments." It named what was happening without euphemism. It condemned what was being done to her. It drew a line Harry knew he might not be able to uncross.

She searched his face, saw the resolve there, the anger he'd been holding back. She wanted to tell him not to do it, that it would make things worse, that the institution would punish them both for stepping out of line. But she also wanted someone, anyone, to stand up and say the truth.

"Are you sure?" she asked.

"I'm sure."

The statement went out a week later. Carefully worded but unmistakable in its intent. Harry condemned the abuse Meghan had been subjected to, called out the racial undertones, demanded that the press show basic decency. The reaction was immediate and divided. Some praised him for defending her. Others accused him of overreacting, of being manipulated, of breaking with royal protocol. The tabloids that had been criticised doubled down, framing the statement as evidence that Meghan was changing him, corrupting him, pulling him away from his family.

Meghan read the responses alone in her apartment, her phone buzzing with messages from friends asking if she was okay. She wasn't. She felt exposed, vulnerable, as though the statement had stripped away the last layer of protection she'd had. But she also felt something else. Gratitude. Relief. The knowledge that Harry had chosen her over the institution's silence.

When he called that night, she answered on the first ring.

"Thank you," she said.

"You don't have to thank me."

"I do. You didn't have to do that."

"Yes, I did." His voice was quiet, steady. "I'm not going to watch you be torn apart and do nothing. I won't be that person."

She closed her eyes, felt the tears coming again. "I love you."

"I love you too. And we'll get through this."

She wanted, needed that. They held each other close.

The engagement happened in November, though the announcement wouldn't come until later. Harry had planned it carefully, choosing a quiet evening at Nott Cott, just the two of them and a roast chicken that was slightly overcooked. He went down on one knee while she was washing dishes, the ring box open in his hand, his expression nervous in a way she'd never seen before.

"Will you marry me?" he asked.

She turned, water still running, her hands covered in soap. For a moment she couldn't speak. Not because she didn't know the answer, but because the question felt enormous. Not just a proposal but a commitment to everything that came with it. The scrutiny. The protocols. The loss of the life she'd built independently. The understanding that she would never again be just Meghan Markle, actress, advocate, woman. She would be part of something larger, older, more powerful than anything she'd ever encountered.

"Yes," she said. "Of course yes."

He slipped the ring onto her finger, stood, pulled her into a kiss. They held on to one another in the small kitchen, the water still running in the sink, the future stretching out before them.

Later, lying in bed, her head on his chest, she felt his heartbeat steady beneath her ear.

"Are you scared?" she asked.

He thought for a second or two. "Yes."

"Me too."

"We don't have to do this. We could walk away, live a completely different life."

She lifted her head, looked at him in the darkness. "Do you want to walk away?"

"No. But I want you to have the choice."

She thought about that. The choice. The word felt almost quaint, as though choice were something simple, something you could make once and be done with.

"I choose this," she said.

"I choose you. And whatever comes with it."

He kissed her forehead and held her closer.

"Then we'll face it together."

She closed her eyes, felt the weight of the ring on her finger. Somewhere beyond the cottage walls, the palace hummed with its ancient machinery. And somewhere further still, millions of people who didn't know her prepared to have opinions about her choices, her suitability, her place in a lineage that stretched back centuries.

But in the quiet of Nott Cott, with Harry's arms around her, she felt a spark of resolve.

She had said yes. And she would mean it.

A meeting was scheduled for two o'clock on a Thursday, tucked between a fitting for an upcoming event and tea with one of Charles's patronages. The calendar entry said only "Discussion re: personal projects" with a name Meghan didn't recognise. She'd assumed it was about coordinating her advocacy work with existing royal initiatives.

She arrived at the office in Kensington Palace with her notebook, ready to discuss how *The Tig*'s platform might amplify causes the family already supported.

The office was exactly what she'd expected. Mahogany desk, photographs of the Queen in silver frames, a clock that ticked with metronomic precision. The woman behind the desk was younger than Meghan anticipated, perhaps 40, with the particular polish that came from years of working inside institutions where presentation mattered more than personality. She stood when Meghan entered, extending her hand.

"Your Royal Highness. Thank you for coming."

Meghan still flinched slightly at the title. It had been hers for only a few weeks, since the engagement announcement, and it sat on her shoulders like borrowed clothing that didn't quite fit. "Of course. Though I'm not entirely sure what we're discussing."

The woman gestured to a chair. Meghan sat. There was tea already poured, biscuits arranged on a plate that looked expensive enough to be historical. Neither of them touched anything.

"We wanted to have a conversation about your online presence," the woman began. "Specifically, your blog. *The Tig.*"

"Right," Meghan said. "I've been thinking about how we might integrate it with royal work. I have a substantial following, and the content aligns with a lot of causes the family supports. Women's issues, education, sustainable fashion. I could—"

"I'm afraid that's not quite what we had in mind."

The interruption was gentle but absolute. Meghan stopped mid-sentence, waiting. The clock ticked. Outside, she could hear the distant sound of a helicopter, probably press, circling at the edge of the restricted airspace.

"The issue," the woman continued, choosing her words with visible care, "is that *The Tig* represents a personal platform. And personal platforms create complications when you're representing the institution. Everything you post, every interview you feature, every product you mention, it all gets scrutinised for political implications, commercial interests, consistency with palace messaging."

"But I'm careful about that already," Meghan said. "I don't endorse products for money. I interview people who are doing meaningful work. The content is thoughtful, not controversial."

"I understand. And the work you've done has been admirable. But the concern isn't about the content you've posted. It's about the content you might post. Or more precisely, the perception that you're acting independently rather than in coordination with the family's communications strategy."

Meghan felt something cold. The concern wasn't about what she'd done. It was about what she might do. About the possibility of her, ungoverned.

"So you're asking me to submit posts for approval before publishing?" she asked.

"We're suggesting that maintaining a personal blog may not be compatible with your new role."

The clock ticked. The tea cooled. Meghan looked at the woman across the desk and understood that this wasn't a meeting where her perspective would alter the outcome. The decision had been made before she walked into the room. This meeting was courtesy. This meeting was notification.

"You want me to close it," Meghan said.

"We think it would be best. The family doesn't maintain personal social media in that way. It creates vulnerabilities."

"It's not just social media. It's years of work. It's my voice. It's how I've connected with people who care about the same things I do."

"I understand it feels like a loss," the woman said. "But you'll have other platforms now. Patronages, speeches, official engagements. Your voice will reach more people than ever before."

"Through official channels. With approved messaging. After it's been edited by people who weren't there, who don't know the communities I've worked with, who are more concerned with protocol than impact."

The woman didn't disagree. She simply waited, her expression unchanged, until the silence itself became answer enough.

Meghan thought about *The Tig*. Five years of building something that was entirely hers. Interviews with women she admired. Essays about travel and food and the small ways people could make their lives more intentional. Advocacy for causes that mattered. She'd written every word herself. Chosen every image. Built a community of readers who trusted her voice because it was authentic, unfiltered, hers. And now, in the palace's view, it was a vulnerability. A complication. Something that appeared to need managing, containing, ultimately eliminating.

"When do you need this to happen?" Meghan asked.

"Before the wedding would be ideal. It creates a clean break between your previous life and your new role."

Previous life. As if everything she'd built before Harry was just prologue. As if her work, her voice, her platform mattered only as things to be left behind.

"Can I think about it?" Meghan asked, already knowing the answer.

"Of course. Though there isn't much to deliberate. The family's position is quite clear."

Meghan stood. The meeting was over. She'd been told what was expected, and now the expectation would sit with her until she complied. The woman stood as well, extending her hand again.

"I know this isn't easy," she said. "But you'll find that letting go of certain things makes space for what comes next."

Meghan couldn't tell whether the woman believed this or was simply delivering a message she'd been instructed to give. Either way, the outcome felt predetermined. She'd walked into a discussion that was actually a notification.

She shook her hand, managed something that approximated a smile, and left. The corridor outside was quiet, just the sound of her heels against marble, the distant murmur of staff in offices she couldn't see. She walked back to Nottingham Cottage, let herself in, and stood in the small living room she'd been trying to make feel like home.

Harry found her there an hour later, sitting on the sofa, laptop open, scrolling through years of posts. Articles about menstrual health in developing countries. Interviews with activists. Essays about finding joy in ordinary moments. Her voice, preserved in pixels, about to be archived into nothing.

"What happened?" he asked, sitting beside her.

She told him. Not with anger, not yet. That would come later. For now, just the facts. The meeting, the decision, the expectation that she'd comply quietly. He listened, his expression darkening.

"We can fight it," he said.

"Can we?"

He hesitated. "I don't know."

She closed the laptop. Looked at him. "This is just the beginning, isn't it?"

He squeezed her hand. Didn't answer because they both already knew.

She would close *The Tig*. She would comply. She would let this part of herself be archived away.

The tiara incident became a flashpoint nobody outside the palace would learn about for years. Meghan wanted to wear a specific tiara for the wedding, Queen Mary's diamond bandeau, and needed a fitting to ensure it worked with her chosen hairstyle. The Queen's dresser, Angela Kelly, was responsible for access to the royal jewels. The fitting was delayed. Then delayed again. Harry, frustrated by what felt like deliberate obstruction, confronted staff directly. Meghan had approached the fitting the way she approached everything, with a schedule, a clear idea of what she needed, and an expectation that logistics would be resolved efficiently. She'd sent multiple follow-up emails when the first request went unanswered, each one more direct than the last. In Los Angeles, in Toronto, this was how things got done. You identified a problem, you chased it, you solved it. But inside the palace, persistence read as entitlement. Following up read as failing to understand your place in the queue. She was asking for something reasonable in a way the institution found unreasonable, and neither side could see the other's logic. "What Meghan wants, Meghan gets," he reportedly said, his patience frayed by months of small resistances accumulating into something larger.

The Queen eventually intervened, the fitting happened, the tiara was worn. But the incident revealed fractures that would only widen. Harry saw an institution making things difficult for his fiancée. The institution saw a prince who'd forgotten his place in the hierarchy, a woman who expected accommodation rather than earning it.

The engagement announcement came in late November, carefully staged photographs released to the press, a brief interview where they smiled and spoke about love and commitment and the future. Meghan wore a white coat, Harry stood close beside her, their hands intertwined, the ring catching light for the cameras. The world reacted exactly as she'd feared it would. Divided. Passionate. Loud.

Some celebrated. Others critiqued. Commentators debated her suitability, her background, her American citizenship, her divorce, her biracial identity. The palace issued statements expressing happiness and support, but the warmth felt performative, the words carefully chosen to sound welcoming without committing to anything substantive.

Meghan moved through the days following the announcement in a strange fog, attending events, meeting people, learning protocols that felt more intricate with each passing week. She met William and Catherine, the encounter polite but formal. She met Charles, who was warmer, more curious, asking about her work and seeming genuinely interested in her answers. She met staff members, advisors, people whose job it was to prepare her for the role she'd agreed to take on.

She arrived with plans. Proposals for patronages she wanted to support, ideas for integrating her advocacy work with royal engagements, spreadsheets outlining timelines and deliverables. She emailed staff at five in the morning, the way she'd always worked, not realising that in this context urgency read as demand, that thoroughness looked like overreach. Staff who were accustomed to months of careful consultation found themselves fielding detailed proposals before they'd finished their first coffee. Some appreciated the energy. Others felt steamrolled. The word "difficult" started circulating before she'd been in the role long enough to understand why.

And through it all, she felt herself changing. Not intentionally, not consciously, but in small ways that accumulated. The way she smiled. The way she stood. The way she chose her words more carefully, aware that everything she said could be misinterpreted, weaponised, turned into headlines. She was becoming more cautious, more guarded, less willing to speak freely.

Harry noticed. He'd catch her staring into space, ask if she was okay. She'd smile, say she was fine, and mean it in the moment.

One evening in December, they sat together at Nott Cott, the fire crackling, snow falling softly outside. Harry was reading something on his phone, his expression distant. Meghan watched him, saw the tension in his shoulders, the way he couldn't sit still as he scrolled. She knew he was reading about her, about them, about the relentless commentary that never seemed to stop.

"Put the phone down," she said gently.

He looked up, managed a smile. "You're right. Sorry."

"It's okay. I know it's hard not to look."

"It shouldn't be this hard. None of this should be this hard."

She moved closer, rested her head on his shoulder. Outside, London was quiet, blanketed in white. Inside, they embraced tightly, two people trying to believe that love would be enough to carry them through whatever came next.

**"'It was just me, me, me': Meghan refers to herself
more than 50 times in seven minutes"**
Rebecca Perring, *Daily Express*, 6 September 2022

6

'(Almost) Straight Outta Compton'

The phone call came at four in the morning, three days before the wedding. Meghan woke to the buzzing on her nightstand, Harry's name glowing on the screen. She answered before her brain had fully caught up to consciousness, her voice thick with sleep.

"What's wrong?"

"It's your father." Harry's voice was tight, controlled in the way it got when he was trying not to lose his temper. "The *Mail* has photos. Staged photos. He's been working with paparazzi."

The photographs showed Thomas at an internet café, looking at pictures of Harry. Thomas reading a book called *Images of Britain*. Thomas being fitted for his wedding suit. All staged, all paid for, all arranged through a paparazzi photographer named Jeff Rayner who'd been tipped off by someone at *TMZ*. Thomas had been in communication with *TMZ* for weeks, feeding them information, coordinating the narrative. His daughter's wedding had become a revenue opportunity.

She sat up, the duvet falling away, cold air hitting her skin. "What kind of photos?"

"Reading a book about British history. Looking at pictures of us on a computer. Getting fitted for a suit. They're clearly set up. He's been paid for them."

The words took a moment to land. Staged photos. Working with paparazzi. Her father. Three days before the wedding. She pressed her palm against her forehead, trying to make the information fit into something that made sense.

"How much?" she asked.

"Does it matter?"

"I need to know."

Harry exhaled. "They're saying over £100,000."

How much? Her father had sold photographs of himself pretending to prepare for her wedding for £100,000. She thought about the conversations they'd had, the plans, his excitement about walking her down the aisle. All of it running parallel to negotiations with tabloid photographers. All of it performance.

She stood, walked to the window of the hotel suite where she'd been staying. London was still dark, the streets empty except for early delivery trucks and the occasional taxi. Somewhere out there, newspapers were being printed with her father's staged photographs. Somewhere, the story was already becoming the story.

She'd been texting him for days, messages that would later be submitted as evidence in her court case. "I've been reaching out to you all weekend but you're not taking any of our calls or replying to any texts," she'd written. "Very concerned about your health and safety and have taken every measure to protect you but I'm not sure what more we can do if you don't respond." The texts showed her trying to help, offering to send someone to be with him, begging him to stop speaking to the press. They also showed him not responding, or responding inconsistently, or making promises he didn't keep.

"Meghan," Harry started.

"I need to talk to him. Now."

She ended the call, scrolled to her father's number, pressed dial. It rang four times before going to voicemail. She tried again. Voicemail. Again. Voicemail. By the fifth attempt, her hands were shaking, anger and panic mixing into something that could just explode. She kept calling. He kept not answering. The sky outside began to lighten.

When Harry arrived at the hotel an hour later, she was sitting on the floor in the bathroom, still in her pyjamas, phone clutched in her hand. The tile was cold against her legs. She'd stopped crying at some point but couldn't remember when. He knelt beside her without speaking, just his presence, solid and steady. She leaned against him, felt his arms come around her.

"He won't answer," she whispered.

"I know."

"Why would he do this? Why would he sell photos three days before the wedding?"

Harry didn't answer because there wasn't an answer, or there were too many answers, none of them good enough to make sense of the betrayal. They sat on the cold tile floor while London woke up outside, while the story spread, while her father's silence grew louder than any explanation could have been.

Her phone buzzed with a text from Jessica Mulroney, who'd been in London for weeks helping with final preparations. "Saw the news. Coming over. Don't argue."

Jessica arrived within the hour, let herself in with the key Meghan had given her, and found them still in the bathroom. She didn't say anything, just sat down on the cold floor with them, her designer clothes meeting the same tiles, and held Meghan's other hand.

"What do you need?" Jessica asked after a long silence.

"I don't know."

"Then I'll stay until you figure it out."

She did stay. Through the morning, through the calls that didn't connect, through the slow accumulation of understanding that her father wasn't coming. Jessica handled logistics Meghan couldn't face, fielded calls from people who didn't need to speak to Meghan directly, made sure someone brought food even if no one ate it. The small acts of friendship that don't make news but that make survival possible.

By evening, the story had metastasised. Thomas Markle had given an interview, claiming he'd staged the photos to improve his image, to show he wasn't just some reclusive man hiding from cameras. Then came the second interview, this one claiming he'd had a heart attack, that he couldn't travel, that he wouldn't be walking his daughter down the aisle. Then a third interview contradicting the second, saying he would come. Then silence.

Meghan sat in a palace office with Harry and two senior aides, everyone's face carefully neutral as they discussed options, contingencies, backup plans. One aide suggested they delay. Another suggested Meghan walk alone. A third mentioned that Charles had offered to step in. The conversation happened around her while she sat very still, her hands folded in her lap, trying to appear composed when what she wanted was to scream.

"What do you want?" Harry asked, cutting through the diplomatic language.

She looked at him. "I want my father to be there. I want him to walk me down the aisle like we planned. I want this to be normal."

"I know. But if he can't come..."

"If he won't come," she corrected. "He's choosing not to come."

The aide across from her shifted uncomfortably. "We can't know that for certain. If he's had a medical episode..."

"He gave three interviews in two days," Meghan said, her voice flat. "He's not in a hospital bed. He's avoiding the consequences of what he's done."

No one argued. The room fell into a silence that felt like acknowledgment.

"Charles's offer stands," the aide said gently. "He would be honoured to walk you down the aisle."

Meghan nodded slowly. "Then yes. Please tell him yes. And thank you."

After the meeting, she and Harry walked through Kensington Gardens, security at a discreet distance, the evening light turning everything gold. Tourists recognised them, pulled out phones, but didn't approach. Just watched, took photos, whispered to each other. Meghan felt their eyes but couldn't find the energy to mind.

"I'm sorry," Harry said.

"You don't have anything to be sorry for."

"Your father," he began.

"Is making his own choices. Bad ones, but his."

The bridesmaid dress fitting had happened that same week, Tuesday afternoon, three days before the wedding. Charlotte and the other flower girls needed final alterations. The dresses had been made to measurements taken weeks earlier, but children grow unpredictably. Some of the hems were wrong. Some fit poorly around the bodice.

Kate had arrived at Kensington Palace with Charlotte, found Meghan and her wedding coordinator discussing adjustments with the seamstress. The tension in the room was immediate, invisible but present. Kate was managing wedding stress for her daughter while Meghan was managing wedding stress for herself while simultaneously processing her father's betrayal which had dominated headlines for days.

Charlotte's dress needed shortening. This much was clear. But the seamstress had limited time, other dresses also needed work, and Kate had specific vision for how it should look. The conversation escalated. Not to shouting, nothing dramatic, just two women under pressure disagreeing about children's clothing when neither had bandwidth for disagreement.

Kate said something about the dress. Meghan, already raw from the Thomas situation, the stress, the exhaustion, heard it differently than perhaps intended. She felt criticised. She felt blamed for dresses not fitting perfectly despite having followed every protocol, used recommended seamstress, done everything the palace way. She fought tears, lost the fight, left the room.

Kate realised immediately she'd misstepped. Not intentionally cruel, just thoughtless timing. She sent flowers the next day with a note apologising. Meghan appreciated the gesture, accepted the apology. They were both under pressure. These things happened. It was minor conflict, quickly resolved, the kind of family friction that occurs at weddings everywhere.

Four months later, The *Telegraph* published a story claiming Meghan had made Kate cry over the dresses. The reverse of what happened. The story spread, was repeated as fact, became one of the key pieces of evidence that Meghan was difficult, demanding, cruel to Kate. The palace had corrected stories about William. About Kate. About Charles. They had staff present at the fitting. They had Kate's flowers and note as evidence. They said nothing.

They stopped near the Round Pond, watching ducks glide across the surface. The water reflected clouds and sky, everything inverted, the world upside down.

"I wanted him there," she said quietly. "I wanted to walk down that aisle with my father beside me. I wanted one part of this day to feel like it belonged to me, to my family, to where I came from."

Harry stroked her hand. "I know."

"And now everyone's going to say he didn't come because he doesn't approve, or because he's ashamed, or because I'm somehow responsible for this mess."

"Let them say whatever they want. You know the truth."

She turned to him, saw the anger in his eyes that he was trying to contain for her sake. "The truth doesn't matter to them. It never has."

"Then we make our own truth. We get married, we build our life, and we don't let anyone else write the story."

She wanted to believe that this crisis could be contained, that her father's choices wouldn't define her wedding, her marriage, her entry into his family. But standing there in the fading light, three days from a wedding the whole world would watch, she felt the story already slipping from her grasp.

The morning of 19 May arrived in a blur of activity that felt both surreal and hyper-real. Meghan woke at 5am, her mother already awake in the adjoining room of the suite, the sound of quiet movement through the walls. Someone brought breakfast neither of them touched. Someone else brought final schedules, timing breakdowns, instructions. Hair and makeup arrived at six. The dress arrived at seven, sheathed in protective fabric, handled with the reverence usually reserved for holy relics.

Doria sat beside her while the hairstylist worked, their hands linked, neither speaking much. What was there to say? The day had its own momentum now, a machine set in motion months ago that wouldn't stop regardless of anyone's feelings about it. Meghan watched her mother's reflection in the mirror, saw the worry behind the calm exterior.

"How are you feeling?" Doria asked.

"Like I'm about to walk into the most scrutinised moment of my life."

"You are."

Meghan laughed despite herself. "You're supposed to say something reassuring."

"I could. But you'd know I was lying." Doria squeezed her hand. "You're going to be fine. You're going to be beautiful. And at the end of all this, you'll be married to a man who loves you. That's what matters."

"Is it enough?"

"I don't know, baby. But it's what you've got."

The honesty steadied her more than any platitude could have. Meghan closed her eyes, let the hairstylist work, tried to quiet her mind enough to simply be present. This was her wedding day. Somewhere beneath the protocols and the cameras and the global audience, this was supposed to be joyful.

The dress was silk cady, simple lines, boat neck, three-quarter sleeves, designed by Clare Waight Keller for Givenchy with an elegance that felt timeless, unfussy, the kind of dress that wouldn't age in photographs. The veil stretched 16 feet, hand-embroidered with the distinctive flora of all 53 Commonwealth countries, a detail that had taken hundreds of hours to perfect. Wintersweet for the gardens of Kensington Palace. California poppies for where she'd grown up. Each flower placed by hand, each representing something specific, the veil itself a statement about the global role she thought she was stepping into. When Meghan saw herself fully dressed, she welled up with tears of pride. She looked like a bride. She looked like herself. The two things didn't feel as mutually exclusive as she'd feared they might.

Her mother's eyes filled with tears. "Oh, Meghan."

"Don't," Meghan said, her own voice unsteady. "If you cry, I'll cry, and then the makeup will be ruined."

Doria laughed, wiped her eyes carefully. "You look perfect. Your father." She stopped, recalibrated. "He should be here. He should see this."

"But he's not. So we move forward without him."

"That's my girl."

The cars arrived at 8.30. Meghan and Doria rode together to Windsor, the streets lined with people behind barriers, flags waving, faces pressed close to catch a glimpse through the tinted windows. The noise was muted but present, a constant hum of excitement and anticipation. Meghan kept her hands folded in her lap, the bouquet beside her, trying to breathe steadily.

"There are a lot of people," Doria said, peering out.

"A few."

"More than a few."

St George's Chapel appeared ahead, Gothic and imposing, tourists and press and security creating layers of controlled chaos. The car pulled up to a private entrance, away from the main crowds. Meghan stepped out carefully, the veil requiring assistance from three people, the dress moving like water. Someone handed her the bouquet. Someone else adjusted the veil. Instructions were murmured about timing, about pacing, about where to stand.

Then she was alone in a small anteroom, just her and Doria and the sound of organ music drifting through stone walls. Her mother straightened the veil one last time, kissed her cheek.

"I love you," Doria said.

"I love you too."

"Go marry your prince."

Meghan smiled, squeezed her mother's hand, then watched her leave to take her seat. The room felt enormous without her. Meghan stood in her dress, in her veil, listening to the music swell, knowing that on the other side of those doors two thousand people waited, along with cameras broadcasting to millions, maybe billions. She thought about her father, wondered if he was watching from California, if he felt regret or just relief at avoiding the spotlight he'd said he wanted to escape.

Then she stopped thinking about him. This was her day. Hers and Harry's. Whatever else it had become, whatever performance was required, at its core was still just two people making a commitment. She could hold onto that.

The doors opened. The music switched to pure processional. The children entered first, the bridesmaids and page boys, small and perfect in their roles. Then the moment arrived. Her moment. The signal was given.

Meghan stepped into the chapel alone.

The aisle stretched impossibly long, light streaming through stained glass, faces turning toward her from both sides. She walked slowly, the veil trailing behind, her hands steady on the bouquet. She kept her eyes forward, aware of Harry at the altar but not looking at him yet, not until she'd covered this distance that felt symbolic of something larger than geography. A woman walking alone into a room full of strangers, carrying herself.

Halfway down the aisle, Charles stepped forward from his seat. He smiled, extended his arm. Meghan took it, grateful for the gesture, for the acknowledgment of what was missing, for his willingness to stand in the gap her father had left. They walked together the rest of the way, her hand on his arm, his presence solid beside her.

When they reached the altar, Charles stepped back. Harry stepped forward. Their eyes met. For a moment, everything else fell away. The cameras, the congregation, the weight of expectation. Just him. Just this. Just the reason she was here.

"Hi," he whispered.

"Hi," she whispered back.

The Archbishop began speaking, his voice carrying through the chapel, words about love and commitment and the sacred nature of marriage. Meghan tried to focus, tried to hear what was being said, but her mind kept drifting. To her father watching somewhere alone. To her mother sitting in the front row, the only member of her family present. To the people outside, the strangers who had woken early to catch a glimpse of her dress, who felt entitled to opinions about her choices.

Bishop Michael Curry, the first African American presiding bishop of the Episcopal Church, delivered a sermon that electrified the chapel and confused the aristocracy. "There's power in love," he preached, his voice rising and falling with the cadences of the black church, quoting Dr Martin Luther King Jr while the congregation shifted in their seats, unused to this kind of energy in royal ceremonies. Some guests looked bewildered. Some looked delighted. The cameras caught it all, the collision of traditions, the monarchy encountering something it hadn't quite prepared for.

The Gospel choir sang *Stand By Me*, Karen Gibson and The Kingdom Choir filling the stone space with warmth and soul, with Los Angeles, with the black church tradition her mother had raised her in. Meghan held her tears back. She glanced at Harry, saw his eyes shining, saw him mouthing the words. He was here. He was present. He loved her. That was enough.

The vows came. She repeated the words, heard her voice echo back from stone walls. For better, for worse. For richer, for poorer. In sickness and in health. The promises felt enormous, impossible to fully grasp in this moment but spoken anyway because that's what faith required. Faith that they could build something lasting. Faith that love was stronger than scrutiny.

Harry slipped the ring on her finger. She slipped his ring on his finger. The Archbishop pronounced them husband and wife. Permission to kiss. Harry leaned in, kissed her softly, respectfully, a kiss for the cameras but also for them. The chapel erupted in applause. The organ piped a triumphant swell. They turned to face the congregation, married now, the Duchess of Sussex, titles bestowed that morning by the Queen.

They walked back down the aisle together, Meghan's hand on Harry's arm, smiling now because the hardest part was over. Outside, the carriage waited, horses in formation, crowds pressing against barriers. She and Harry climbed in, the door closing behind them, and suddenly they were moving through Windsor, through streets lined with thousands of people waving flags and cheering.

Meghan waved back, her smile genuine now, caught up in the sheer energy of it all. She looked at Harry, saw him grinning, saw his relief that they'd made it through. She laughed, sudden and bright, and he laughed too, and for a few minutes it felt exactly like what it was supposed to be. A celebration. A beginning. Two people starting a life together.

"We did it," he said.

"We did."

"You were perfect."

"So were you."

He kissed her again, longer this time, no cameras inside the carriage to perform for. Just them. Just this moment before they returned to the palace, to the reception, to more photographs and speeches.

The carriage rounded a corner, more crowds, more cheering. Meghan waved, felt the surreality settle over her again. This morning she'd been Meghan Markle. Now she was the Duchess of Sussex. The same person, but different. Forever changed by this day.

After the carriage procession, Harry drove them to the evening reception at Frogmore House in a silver-blue Jaguar E-Type, converted to electric, the two of them alone for the first time all day. The car was borrowed, iconic, the kind of vehicle that made photographers lean forward. Meghan had changed into a second dress by then, Stella McCartney, silk and elegant, more comfortable for moving, a halter neck in lily white that moved like water when she walked. The room was filled with faces she was beginning to recognise, Harry's friends who'd become her friends, colleagues from *Suits* who'd flown across an ocean to be there, her mother seated near the front, finally able to relax now that the formal ceremony had passed.

Charles gave a speech that surprised her with its warmth. He spoke about Harry's happiness, about the joy of watching his son find someone who brought out the best in him, about welcoming Meghan into the family. His voice carried genuine affection, and when he made a joke about Harry's cooking skills, the room laughed with the ease of people who weren't performing.

George Clooney appeared beside her at one point, glass of champagne in hand, asking if she was surviving the overwhelming nature of the day. They'd met through mutual friends, and his presence felt like a bridge between her old life and this new one.

"You did great," he said. "And for what it's worth, I've been to a lot of weddings. This one actually felt real."

"It is real," she said. "That's what I keep trying to remember."

"Good. Hold onto that. The rest of it," he gestured vaguely at the grandeur surrounding them, "is just set dressing."

Serena found her later, pulled her into a hug that lasted longer than ceremony required.

"I'm so proud of you," Serena said. "Look what you've done."

"I just got married. People do it every day."

"No. You walked into a room full of people who've been doing this for centuries and you held your own. That takes something."

Meghan felt tears threaten again, blinked them back. "I couldn't have done it without you. All of you. Everyone who came."

"That's the point. You don't have to do anything alone."

The evening stretched into night, dancing and laughter and moments that would become photographs in albums. Harry held her close during their first dance, his hand steady on her back, his voice low in her ear.

"We actually did it," he said.

"We actually did."

"Whatever comes next, we have today."

She looked at him, at the face she'd chosen to spend her life with, and felt something settle in her chest. Not certainty exactly, but resolve. They would face whatever came. Together.

Later, much later, when they were finally alone in their room, the dress carefully hung, the veil folded, the day finished, Meghan sat on the edge of the bed and felt the weight of everything settle. Harry came out of the bathroom, saw her face, sat beside her without speaking.

"What is it?" he asked gently.

She tried to find words for the feeling. The sense that something had changed today, something irrevocable. That she'd crossed a threshold that had closed behind her. That the life she'd known before was now officially over. She was part of this institution now. Bound to it in ways she was only beginning to understand.

"I'm just tired," she said finally.

He embraced her gently, and she let herself lean into him, let herself be held. Tomorrow they'd wake up as Duke and Duchess, with new responsibilities, new expectations, new pressures. But tonight, they could just be two people who had promised to love each other, whatever the future held.

Outside, Windsor slept. Inside, Meghan closed her eyes, felt Harry's heartbeat steady beneath her ear, and tried to believe that this, at least, would be enough. The promises made today. The love that had brought them here.

She wanted, needed to believe it. Even as a small voice whispered that the hardest parts were still ahead.

**"Not long to go! Pregnant Kate tenderly cradles her
baby bump while wrapping up her royal duties
ahead of maternity leave"**
Rebecca English, *Daily Mail* Royal Correspondent, 21 March 2018

.

"Why can't Meghan Markle keep her hands off her bump?
Experts tackle the question that has got the nation talking:
Is it pride, vanity, acting or a new age bonding technique?"
Mail on Sunday reporter, 26 January 2019

7

'Meghan Made Kate Cry'

The honeymoon lasted three days. Not the official one, there would be time for that later, but the brief window when being newly married felt more significant than being newly royal. They stayed at a private estate in the Cotswolds, sleeping late, cooking meals that burned slightly at the edges, walking through fields where no one recognised them. Meghan wore Harry's jumpers. Harry made tea that was too strong. They talked about the wedding, about the moments that had felt real beneath the performance, about her father's absence in a way they hadn't had time to properly process before.

On the third morning, Harry's phone rang. A private secretary, calling about schedules, about engagements that needed confirming, about the machinery resuming its usual rhythm. The honeymoon ended the moment he answered. Meghan watched his face change as he listened, watched the husband become the prince again, watched the brief pocket of ordinary life seal itself shut.

They returned to London, to Kensington Palace, to Nottingham Cottage that suddenly felt smaller than before. Wedding gifts were still arriving, stacked in the hall, cards from strangers expressing joy and support and sometimes thinly veiled criticism. Meghan opened them methodically, writing thank you notes in her careful handwriting, aware that even gratitude required protocol.

The engagements began immediately. Walkabouts, charity visits, receptions where she stood beside Harry and smiled at people whose names she'd forget by evening. She watched how Harry moved through crowds, how he knew instinctively when to linger and when to move on, how he could make brief exchanges feel meaningful without ever revealing anything real. She tried to learn. Tried to absorb through observation what he'd learned through a lifetime of practice.

"You're doing brilliantly," he told her after a particularly long day in Chester.

"I'm exhausted."

"That's normal. It does get easier."

Already she could feel the toll, the way her face ached from smiling, the way her feet screamed in heels chosen for photographs rather than comfort, the way she returned to Nott Cott each evening and collapsed on the sofa, too drained to cook, too wired to sleep.

The headlines continued their relentless assessment. What she wore, how she wore it, whether she touched her hair too much or smiled too little or stood too close to Harry or not close enough. Every gesture dissected, every choice questioned. The rules were unwritten but the violations were published daily.

The coverage of both pregnancies revealed the pattern clearly. When Kate touched her bump in public photographs, the caption read "Proud Mum Kate." When Meghan did exactly the same thing at exactly the same stage of pregnancy, the caption read "Why Can't Meghan Keep Her Hands Off Her Bump?" The photographs were nearly identical. The framing was entirely different.

Kate eating avocados, "Kate's Superfood Secret." Meghan eating avocados, "Meghan's Favourite Food Linked to Human Rights Abuses."

Kate closing a car door herself, "Duchess Shows She's Normal." Meghan closing a car door herself, "Duchess Defies Protocol."

In July, they visited Ireland. Two days of engagements, carefully planned, perfectly executed. They met with young entrepreneurs, visited cultural sites, attended a garden party at the British Ambassador's residence. Meghan spoke about the importance of empowering young women, about education, about opportunity. But the coverage focused on her dress touching Harry's back during a photo, on whether her skirt was too short, on speculation about tension between her and palace staff. Nothing she actually said made the headlines. Just her body, her clothes, her perceived infractions against unwritten rules.

"How do you stand it?" she asked Harry on the flight home.

"I don't read it."

"But you know it's there."

"I've learned to separate what's real from what's performed. They're writing fiction about us. It doesn't change who we actually are."

She looked out the window at clouds passing below, tried to adopt his philosophy. But fiction repeated often enough became truth in people's minds.

One evening, after another round of headlines that went unchallenged, Harry sat very still on the sofa, his expression shifting through something that looked like revelation.

"I've been seeing this my whole life," he said slowly. "But I've never seen it from outside before."

"What do you mean?"

"The way it works. The leaks. The briefings. The way stories appear that serve someone's interests and there's never any accountability. I thought it was just how things were. I didn't understand it was a system. A system I was part of."

Meghan didn't respond. She just waited.

"When it was happening to me, I could explain it away. But watching it happen to you..." He shook his head. "Familiarity makes you blind. I'm only seeing clearly because I'm watching you see it for the first time."

The Australia tour was announced for October. Sixteen days, four countries, 76 engagements. The most extensive tour they'd done, the first major international trip as a married couple. Meghan prepared meticulously, reading briefings, learning about the organisations they'd visit, practicing names and titles until they felt natural in her mouth.

The morning they left, she felt nauseated. Jet lag, she thought. Stress. The usual physical manifestation of too much pressure. But the nausea persisted through the flight, through their arrival in Sydney, through the first day of engagements. By the second morning, standing in the bathroom of Admiralty House while Harry slept, she took the test she'd brought, just in case.

Two lines.

Pregnant.

She sat on the edge of the bathtub, holding the test, trying to process what it meant. Joy, yes. Fear, absolutely. They'd talked about children, about wanting a family, but not yet, not this soon, not while everything still felt so precarious. But here it was. Cells dividing, a future taking shape, another life tied to theirs and to everything that came with being part of this family.

When she told Harry, he lifted her off the ground, spun her carefully, laughed with a brightness she hadn't heard in weeks. They held each other in the early Sydney morning, aware that this changed everything and aware that they couldn't announce it yet, couldn't let anyone know until they'd made it through the tour, through the first trimester, through the careful protocols around royal pregnancy announcements.

The call from the palace communications office came while they were getting ready for the Melbourne walkabout. Meghan had her hair half done, the stylist working quickly because they were already running five minutes behind schedule. Harry answered his phone in the bathroom, his voice muffled through the door. When he emerged, his expression startled her.

"What?" she asked.

"The *Mail*'s running something. About your father again. They're saying you've abandoned him, that you're heartless."

Meghan met Harry's eyes in the mirror. "Did they ask the palace to comment?"

"Yes."

"And?"

"They're not responding. Standard policy on family matters."

The room fell quiet. She'd learned months ago that protection had limits. But this was different. This was active choice. The story would run unchallenged. Her father's version would stand as truth. And she'd walk out into crowds of Australian well-wishers with that knowledge pressing down on her.

"We need to go," someone said from the doorway. "The crowds are waiting."

The car ride to the walkabout site took twelve minutes. Harry held her hand the entire time. Neither of them spoke. Security briefed them on the route, the timing, the exits. Standard information that washed over her without sticking.

The car stopped. The door opened. Sound rushed in. Thousands of voices, cameras clicking, the particular energy of crowds who'd been waiting for hours in Australian heat. Meghan stepped out into sunshine that felt aggressive, brightness that made her eyes water. She smiled. The smile felt like it belonged to someone else.

The barriers stretched along the waterfront, people pressed three and four deep, phones raised, flowers extended, voices calling her name. She moved along the line with practised ease, shaking hands, accepting bouquets, crouching to speak to children who'd been lifted onto parents' shoulders for better views. The responses were automatic now. "Thank you so much." "How lovely." "What beautiful flowers." Words that served only to fill the space between one person and the next.

A woman in her sixties handed her a small stuffed kangaroo. "For the baby," she said, smiling warmly. "Congratulations."

Meghan's hand went instinctively to her stomach, still flat enough that the pregnancy wasn't visible. "Thank you. That's very kind."

"You'll be a wonderful mum. Don't let them tell you otherwise."

The comment landed strangely. Meghan started to respond, but the woman had already moved back into the crowd, replaced by a teenage girl wanting a photograph. She posed, smiled, moved on. But the words stayed with her. Don't let them tell you otherwise. What had the woman read? What narrative was already forming?

Further along the barrier, a phone was thrust toward her face, someone taking video, and she saw herself on the screen for a split second. Smiling, waving, the image of royal grace. She looked happy. She looked fine. The disconnect between image and reality felt vast enough to fall into.

The walkabout was scheduled for 30 minutes. They stretched it to 40 because the crowds were enthusiastic and cutting it short would seem rude. By the time they reached the end of the barrier line, Meghan's face ached from smiling. Her hand was cramping from being shaken. The flowers had left pollen stains on her dress.

Back in the car, the door closing felt like physical relief.

The noise cut off. The performance could pause.

"You okay?" Harry asked quietly.

"No."

He didn't push. Just held her hand again while the car navigated away from the waterfront.

At Admiralty House, she went straight to the bathroom, locked the door, sat on the edge of the tub. Her phone showed 17 new messages. Friends asking if she was okay. Her mother saying she loved her. Someone from her old *Suits* cast saying the story was rubbish and everyone knew it.

But everyone didn't know it. The story would be read by millions who didn't know her, who'd absorb it as fact, who'd add it to the growing file of evidence that she was cold, calculating, cruel to her own father.

She heard Harry's voice through the door. "Meg?"

She unlocked it, let him in. He looked at her face, saw what she'd been holding back, and pulled her against his chest without speaking. She let herself cry for exactly two minutes. Then she pulled back, wiped her eyes, looked at him.

"How do we survive this?" she asked.

He didn't have an answer. Neither did she. They only had another half an hour before someone knocked on the door to tell them it was time to get ready for the next appearance.

She looked at her reflection. Fixed her makeup. Prepared to go back out.

So she smiled.

They moved from Nottingham Cottage to Frogmore Cottage in early 2019, officially to have more space for the coming baby, unofficially to put distance between themselves and Kensington Palace. The cottage required significant renovation, £2.4 million from the Sovereign Grant, money that would become a point of contention and that Harry and Meghan would later repay in full. The move was read by some as necessary nesting, by others as evidence of the rift with William and Kate, by still others as Meghan's desire for separation from the family she'd married into. All three readings contained truth.

The tour itself was gruelling. Four countries in 16 days, multiple engagements daily, smiling through exhaustion and morning sickness that lasted all day. In quieter moments, Harry would talk about his mother, about Diana's tours, about the parallels he was seeing that terrified him. The same hunting energy from photographers. The same fabricated narratives. The same institutional indifference to someone drowning in public.

"She told people she was struggling," he said one night in their hotel room, Meghan already in bed, too exhausted to move. "She told them she needed help. They did nothing. And I'm watching it happen again."

"I'm not your mother," Meghan said gently.

"I know. But they're treating you the same way they treated her. And I won't let it end the same way."

She didn't ask what he meant by "end." They both knew.

Meghan moved through it with determination, shaking hands, accepting flowers, listening to speeches, delivering her own remarks with careful attention to tone and content.

In Fiji, they visited a market, the air thick with humidity, crowds pressing close despite security. Someone shoved, and in that half-second, Meghan felt genuine fear, the crush of bodies, the awareness of being pregnant and vulnerable. Harry's hand found hers, steadied her, and they made it through, smiling for cameras. But that night, she lay awake in the hotel room, hand on her stomach, understanding with new clarity what she'd signed up for.

The pregnancy announcement came on the first day of the tour, carefully timed by the palace. The reaction was immediate and divided. Congratulations mixed with speculation about timing, about whether she'd planned it to coincide with the tour, about whether she was trying to upstage other family members.

"They're happy for us," Harry insisted. "Most people are happy for us."

"Most people don't write the headlines."

By the time they returned to London in early November, Meghan was exhausted in a way that sleep couldn't fix.

In December 2018, six months after the wedding, a story appeared claiming she'd made Kate cry during a bridesmaid dress fitting before the wedding. The story was false, the reverse of what had actually happened, but it spread quickly, repeated across platforms, treated as fact. Valentine Low would later document how the story had been planted, palace sources actively briefing journalists with a version of events that protected Kate at Meghan's expense. The briefing culture worked exactly as designed. Favoured royals were shielded. Disfavoured ones were exposed.

Meghan waited for the palace to correct it, to issue a statement, to protect her the way they'd protected other family members from false stories. The protection never came.

"They're not going to say anything," Harry told her, his voice tight with frustration. What Meghan didn't know then was that Jason Knauf had already filed his email to Simon Case, documenting the "bullying" allegations that would surface years later at the most damaging possible moment. The institution was keeping records. Building files. Creating a paper trail that could be deployed when needed.

"Why not? It's not true."

"They don't correct stories about family members. It's policy."

"But they've corrected stories before. I've seen them do it."

He didn't answer, and in his silence she understood. They corrected stories about some family members. Not about her.

There were things she wanted to say. Clarifications that would have set the record straight, explanations that would have provided context. But each time she drafted a response, someone advised against it. Don't engage. Don't give them more material. Don't let them see it's working.

So she said nothing. And in saying nothing, she felt pieces of herself go quiet too. The person who had once spoken up about dish soap commercials and called schools about forms was learning a different lesson now, that some situations punished honesty more than silence, and survival required choosing which battles deserved your voice.

She wasn't sure she liked who she was becoming. But she was still becoming her. That was something.

Christmas at Sandringham felt like performance art. The whole family together, traditions observed with careful precision, everyone on their best behaviour for the cameras stationed outside church. Meghan smiled, walked beside Harry, wore the coat and hat chosen for maximum photograph appeal. But inside the house, away from public view, she felt the coolness, the assessment, the sense of being tolerated rather than welcomed.

Jason Knauf had been their communications secretary since before the engagement, a former Treasury press officer brought in to manage media relations for the young royals. He was present for the early tensions, the long hours, the 5am emails that would later become evidence in accusations against Meghan. In October 2018, he emailed Simon Case, then Prince William's private secretary, documenting concerns about Meghan's treatment of staff. The email described a "bullying" pattern, alleged that two personal assistants had been "humiliated" and that the behaviour was "totally unacceptable."

Knauf's email wasn't made public until 2021, when *The Times* obtained it days before the Oprah interview aired.

By then, Knauf had left royal employment. He would later provide testimony against Meghan in her lawsuit against the *Mail on Sunday*, a former employee appearing in court to undermine someone he'd once worked to protect.

Staff departures began being reported. A private secretary leaving, then another assistant, each departure framed as evidence that Meghan was impossible to work for. The stories cited anonymous sources, painted her as demanding and difficult, as someone who reduced people to tears with her expectations. The 5am emails became a particular focus, presented as evidence of unreasonable demands, of someone who didn't understand boundaries. What the stories didn't mention was that 5am emails were standard practice for anyone trying to function across multiple time zones, that American working hours didn't align with British ones, that what looked like demanding behaviour to staff accustomed to palace pace looked like ordinary efficiency to someone who'd spent years in entertainment industry schedules.

The email arrived one Thursday afternoon in February. Meghan was at her desk in Nottingham Cottage, reviewing briefing papers for an upcoming engagement, when the notification appeared. Subject line: "Resignation - Melissa Toubati."

Melissa. Her personal assistant. The woman who'd been with her for six months, who knew her schedule better than Meghan did, who'd seemed competent and professional. Meghan clicked the email open, scanning the formal language. Effective immediately. Grateful for the opportunity. Pursuing other interests.

No phone call. No conversation. Just an email on a Thursday afternoon, leaving her without an assistant two days before a major engagement.

Meghan walked downstairs to find Harry in the kitchen, making tea. "Melissa just quit."

He turned, kettle in hand. "What?"

"Email resignation. Effective immediately."

"Did she say why?"

"Pursuing other interests." Meghan leaned against the counter. "That's the third person in four months."

"They're overworked. Palace staffing levels are ridiculous."

"That's not what the stories will say." She pulled out her phone, already knowing what she'd find, and there it was. The first article, posted 15 minutes ago. "Palace Source: Meghan Markle's Third Aide Quits Amid Claims of 'Difficult' Behaviour."

Harry set down the kettle, came to read over her shoulder. "They don't waste time."

"They had it ready. Someone told them she was quitting before she even sent the email." Meghan scrolled through the article, each paragraph more damaging than the last. Anonymous sources describing a demanding work environment. Claims of early-morning emails, last-minute changes, unreasonable expectations.

"None of that is true," Harry said.

"Doesn't matter. It's out there now."

She walked to the window, looked out at Kensington Palace grounds. Staff members moved between buildings, going about their work. Somewhere in those buildings, someone had called a journalist. Someone had shared Melissa's resignation before Meghan even knew about it. Someone had framed the story to make her the problem.

The next morning, another article appeared. "Meghan Markle Aide Tells Friends: 'I Couldn't Take It Anymore.'" More anonymous sources. More claims about demanding behaviour.

Meghan read it in bed, Harry still sleeping beside her, morning light filtering through the curtains. She thought about the woman she'd worked with for six months, who'd seemed fine, who'd never indicated dissatisfaction. Had she been miserable? Had Meghan missed signs? Or was this just convenient narrative?

Harry woke, saw her with her phone. "More articles?"

"They're saying she was miserable. That I drove her away."

"Did she ever say she was unhappy?"

"No. But maybe she was good at hiding it. Or maybe I was bad at seeing it." She set down the phone, rubbed her eyes. "I don't know anymore. I don't know if I'm actually difficult or if they've just said it enough times that it's become true regardless of reality."

"You're not difficult. You're competent. You're direct. You expect excellence because you demand it of yourself first. That's not the same as being difficult."

"Try telling that to the palace machinery."

Archie was born on 6 May 2019. Early morning, Portland Hospital, just the two of them and medical staff. No press. No announcement until hours later. They'd fought for that privacy, for the chance to meet their son without cameras waiting outside. The palace had resisted, argued for tradition, but Harry had held firm. This moment belonged to them.

Holding Archie for the first time, Meghan felt love, overwhelming and immediate. But also fear. This tiny person would grow up watched, judged, defined by circumstances he hadn't chosen. She looked at Harry, saw the same fear reflected in his face.

The presentation of Archie to the press happened two days later, carefully staged in Windsor Castle.

The christening was scheduled for July, private ceremony at Windsor Castle chapel. Harry and Meghan decided they wouldn't release the names of godparents. This was their choice to make, they reasoned. Archie was seventh in line to the throne, far enough removed that every detail didn't require public consumption. They wanted to protect their friends' privacy, to have something that belonged to them rather than to the institution.

The reaction was immediate and hostile. How dare they keep godparents secret. Who did they think they were. The British public paid for their lives, deserved to know everything. Commentators declared it unprecedented, disrespectful, proof that Meghan was changing Harry into someone secretive and un-British. Never mind that other royals had kept godparents private. Never mind that the ceremony itself was personal rather than state function. The rules were different for the Sussexes. Privacy they tried to maintain became evidence of arrogance.

They released two official photographs. Archie in Meghan's arms, surrounded by family. Doria there, radiant. Charles and Camilla, William and Kate, Diana's sisters. A family portrait that looked warm, genuine, the sort of picture any family might take at a christening. But the limited release became another grievance. Only two photos. No press access to the ceremony. Meghan was controlling the narrative again, being difficult again, refusing to play by rules she'd agreed to by marrying into the family.

The christening gown was traditional, the same replica worn by royal babies for decades. The archbishop of Canterbury performed the ceremony. Every protocol was followed except the one about making godparents public and allowing press documentation of private family moments. That deviation was treated as fundamental breach, proof that the Sussexes wanted royal privilege without royal obligation.

Meghan wore a white dress, stood beside Harry, held their son while cameras flashed. She smiled, answered bland questions about how wonderful it all was.

The "Straight Outta Compton" headline had appeared in *The Sun* when they announced their relationship. Harry's girlfriend described using language referencing the NWA album, black Los Angeles neighborhoods, gangs and violence. The headline made readers think of guns and crime when seeing Meghan's name.

The *Mail* ran a piece titled "Harry's Girl is (Almost) Straight Outta Compton." The modifier "almost" was doing a lot of work.

Meghan had grown up in Los Angeles, yes, but not in Compton or in poverty. Later headlines were no less subtle. "Exotic." "Unusual background." "Different heritage."

The criticism started immediately. She'd held him wrong. She'd stood wrong. The dress was wrong. Nothing she did satisfied the voices that had decided she was the problem.

Maternity leave lasted six weeks. Then back to work, engagements resuming, the performance required even as she navigated sleepless nights and nursing and the ordinary chaos of new motherhood.

In September, they were assigned the Africa tour. Ten days, multiple countries, a documentary crew following them to capture the work for a television special.

The tour began in Cape Town, Archie travelling with them, staying with his nanny at the residence while they visited organisations supporting gender equality and education. Meghan felt more alive than she had in months, talking to women who were fighting for change, hearing stories that reminded her why any of this mattered. For brief moments, she forgot about cameras and focused on connection, on substance, on the work itself.

On the second day, during an engagement in Nyanga township, the heater in Archie's room malfunctioned. Smoke filled the nursery. The nanny smelled it, grabbed Archie, got him out. He was fine. Shaken but unharmed. The nanny had moved him seconds before the heater could have caused serious injury.

Meghan and Harry were told after the engagement, in the car returning to the residence. Their son had nearly been hurt. The room had filled with smoke. If the nanny had been even slightly less vigilant, if she'd left him sleeping just a few minutes longer, the outcome could have been catastrophic.

"We need to cancel tomorrow," Meghan said immediately,
"I need to be with him."

"The schedule is set," someone from the communications team responded. "It can't be changed."

"Our son nearly died."

"But he didn't. He's fine. The engagement tomorrow is important. You can't cancel."

Meghan looked at Harry, saw the same fury she felt reflected in his face. But they were on tour. Official visit. Royal duties. The show must continue regardless of what happened behind the scenes. They'd signed up for this. They were expected to perform.

They went to the next engagement. Meghan smiled, shook hands, gave a speech about women's empowerment that felt like it was coming from someone else's mouth. Her mind was with Archie. Her body was going through motions. The separation between the two felt vast, cruel, evidence of a system that valued appearance over humanity.

That night, she held Archie for hours, breathing in the smell of his hair, feeling his solid warmth against her chest. He was fine. The nanny had saved him. But the "what if" sat heavy. What if she'd been slower? What if the smoke had been thicker? What if they'd lost him because they'd been performing duties for an institution that wouldn't even let them cancel an engagement when their child's safety had been compromised?

"We can't keep doing this," she told Harry that night, after Archie was finally asleep.

"I know."

"I mean it. We can't stay in a system that expects us to smile for cameras hours after our son nearly died."

"I know," he repeated. "I'm trying to figure out how to leave."

But the exhaustion was cumulative. Months of scrutiny, of false stories, of silence while she was torn apart in the press. Months of performing happiness while struggling to survive. By the time the documentary crew asked if she was okay, she'd stopped being able to maintain the façade. The question came from Tom Bradby, *ITV* journalist who'd known Harry for years, who'd covered the royal family with more thoughtfulness than most. They were sitting in a courtyard in Cape Town, the interview winding down, and he'd asked almost casually. "Are you okay?"

The question landed differently than expected. Not the usual "how are you enjoying the tour" but actual concern about her wellbeing. Something broke in her composure. Tears came before she could stop them.

"Not many people have asked if I'm okay," she said, voice breaking. "But it's a very real thing to be going through behind the scenes."

"And the answer is, would it be fair to say, not really okay?" Bradby pressed gently. "That it's really been a struggle?"

She nodded, unable to speak for a moment. "Yes."

The footage went viral within hours of airing. "Not many people have asked if I'm okay" became headline, meme, cultural reference point. Some people watched with empathy, saw a woman genuinely struggling, recognised the loneliness of suffering while everyone assumes you're fine because you're smiling publicly. Others mocked it. Poor princess complaining about her privileged life. Meghan playing victim again. How dare she suggest she wasn't okay when she had wealth, title, beautiful baby, handsome husband.

Harry watched her watch the reaction, saw the way each dismissive comment landed. "They'll never understand," he said.

"I know. But I needed to say it. I needed someone to ask and I needed to answer honestly, just once."

The clip became the most-played moment of the documentary. Not the work they'd done. Not the organisations they'd visited. Just those few seconds of visible pain, of someone too exhausted to maintain composure.

The vulnerability made people uncomfortable. Royals weren't supposed to crack publicly. Meghan had cracked. For some viewers, that made her human. For others, it made her unsuitable. But everyone agreed it was the most honest moment the royal family had allowed cameras to capture in decades.

Harry's portion of the interview was equally raw. He spoke about his mother, about the similarities he saw between what Diana had endured and what Meghan was experiencing. The hunting by paparazzi. The fabricated stories. The racism Diana had faced when dating Dodi Fayed, the headlines comparing her to Mohammed Al-Fayed's family in language that left little to the imagination. The palace's failure to protect her, to correct false narratives, to do anything except watch while the press destroyed her.

"My mother was chased to her death while she was in a relationship with someone who wasn't white," he said, his voice tight with controlled anger. "And now it's happening again. The same people who killed her are going after my wife. The same institution that failed to protect her has failed to protect Meghan. I wasn't old enough to help my mother. I wasn't in a position to do anything about it. But I'm older now. I have a choice. And I choose to prioritise my family's safety over anything else."

When the documentary aired in October, the reaction split predictably. Some people saw two people struggling under impossible pressure, saw the humanity beneath the titles. Others saw weakness, saw complaining, saw privileged people who didn't appreciate what they had.

Meghan watched the documentary alone in their room at Frogmore Cottage, Harry putting Archie to bed. She saw herself on screen, vulnerable in ways she'd tried never to be publicly, and felt exposed. But she also felt something else. The truth was out there now. She'd said what she'd been feeling. Maybe it wouldn't change anything, but at least it existed.

Harry came in, sat beside her on the bed. "You okay?"

She almost laughed. The question that had started everything. "I don't know anymore."

They held hands and sat in silence while the documentary played on.

That night, lying in bed, she felt the breaking point arrive. Not dramatically, not with any single event pushing them over the edge. Just the accumulation of everything, finally exceeding what could be carried. They couldn't keep living like this. Something had to change.

"What if we left?" she whispered.

Harry was quiet for so long she thought he'd fallen asleep. Then his hand covered hers, his voice rough. "I've been thinking the same thing."

"Really?"

"Yeah. I don't see how we survive if we stay."

She closed her eyes. Relief and fear mixed so thoroughly she couldn't separate them.

"What would we do? Where would we go?"

"I don't know. But we'd figure it out."

They lay there in the darkness, their son sleeping down the hall, the institution they'd tried so hard to serve humming around them. Somewhere a decision was forming, not yet fully articulated but already inevitable. The cost of staying had become higher than the cost of leaving.

**"Revealed: The letter showing true tragedy
of Meghan's rift with father"**
Mail on Sunday, 10 February 2019

8

'Sources Say'

The letter had been private. Written in August 2018, shortly after the wedding, when Meghan still believed words could bridge the gap her father had created. Five pages, handwritten, careful. She'd poured everything into it. The hurt of his staged photographs. The betrayal of his tabloid interviews. Her desperate wish for him to stop speaking to the press, to meet his grandson, to repair what he'd broken. She'd written it alone at Nottingham Cottage, tears smudging the ink in places, Harry reading over her shoulder, both of them hoping this might be the thing that changed everything. Her father had received it. Read it. Then photocopied it and sold it to the *Mail on Sunday*.

Meghan learned about the publication on a Sunday morning in February 2019, still in bed at Frogmore Cottage, Archie asleep in the next room. Harry brought her the paper, his face carefully showing little emotion as he tried to protect her from the unavoidable. She read the headline first. "Revealed: The letter showing true tragedy of Meghan's rift with a father she says has 'broken her heart into a million pieces.'"

They'd published excerpts. Carefully selected sentences ripped from context, arranged to paint her as cold, ungrateful, ashamed of her family. They'd even analysed her handwriting, hired a graphologist to declare what her penmanship revealed about her character. The most private thing she'd written, the most vulnerable she'd been on paper, turned into entertainment for millions of Sunday morning readers.

She read it twice. Then she set the paper down very carefully on the duvet and stared at the ceiling. Harry sat beside her, not speaking, just present. After a long silence, she said quietly, "He gave them my letter."

"I know."

"My father sold a letter I wrote begging him to stop selling stories."

"I know."

She turned to look at him, feeling something beyond grief.

"I want to sue."

Harry's brow furrowed. "The palace won't support that."

"I don't care what the palace supports. He stole my letter. They published it. That's not legal."

"It's a fight. A long one. It'll keep this story alive for months, maybe years."

"Then let it. I'm done letting people take things from me with zero consequences."

She meant it. Every word. By then, weeks had become months. She'd waited for someone else to correct the record. No one did. The institution had taught her to absorb attacks silently, to turn the other cheek, to let time and discretion solve problems that required confrontation. But this was her handwriting on those pages. Her pain commodified for profit. Her father's final betrayal made public in the worst possible way. Silence wasn't protection anymore. It was complicity.

The legal implications went beyond copyright.

Jason Knauf, Meghan's former communications secretary, had provided evidence to Associated Newspapers. Text messages. Emails. His testimony suggested Meghan had known her father might share the letter, that she'd written it with public consumption in mind. The palace had initially said they wouldn't cooperate with the lawsuit. But Knauf had provided materials anyway, appearing to support the *Mail*'s defence.

The betrayal was multi-layered. Knauf had worked for her. Had seen the toll the press was taking. Had witnessed the institution's failure to protect her. And when she'd finally fought back through legal means, he'd sided with the tabloid.

His testimony would become central to the *Mail*'s defence, painting her letter as calculated rather than desperate, strategic rather than sincere.

"Why would he do that?" Meghan asked when her lawyers explained Knauf's involvement.

"Several possible reasons. Loyalty to the institution rather than to you personally. Belief that your lawsuit damages the palace's relationship with the press. Instructions from senior staff. We can't know his motivations. We only know what he's provided."

Harry's jaw tightened. "He was supposed to work for us."

"He worked for the institution. You were his assignment. There's a difference."

The distinction was clarifying. They'd spent years believing palace staff worked for them, represented their interests, advocated on their behalf. But the staff served the institution first. When institutional interests and their interests diverged, the staff chose the institution. Every time.

The legal team came to Frogmore that afternoon. Two lawyers, serious and thorough, laying out options and risks. They could pursue a case for copyright infringement, for misuse of private information. The *Mail on Sunday* would fight it. The process would be expensive, exhausting, public. Every detail would be litigated in court and in the press. Her father might be called to testify. Her relationship with him would be dissected in legal filings and newspaper columns.

"But can we win?" Meghan asked.

The senior lawyer, a woman named Jenny, looked at her steadily. "I believe so. They published your private correspondence without permission. They edited it to change its meaning. The law is clear."

"Then I want to proceed."

Harry squeezed her hand. The lawyers made notes, began the machinery of litigation. After they left, Meghan walked through Frogmore's rooms, touching walls, trying to ground herself. She had crossed a line today. Chosen confrontation over compliance. The palace would be furious. The press would frame her as litigious, difficult, aggressive. But at least she was fighting back.

The palace reaction came within 24 hours. A meeting requested, urgent, at Kensington Palace. Meghan and Harry drove there together, silent in the car, both knowing what was coming. They were ushered into an office, two senior communications staff waiting, expressions carefully neutral.

"We understand you've retained legal counsel," the older one said. "Regarding the letter."

"Yes," Meghan replied. "The *Mail on Sunday* had no right to publish it."

"While we understand your frustration, we're concerned about the optics. Legal action draws more attention to the story, keeps it in the news cycle. The preferred approach would be to let it pass quietly."

"Pass quietly while my private correspondence is analysed in newspapers? While my father makes money from betraying me?"

"We know it's difficult. But engaging legally often escalates rather than resolves."

Harry leaned forward. "So what's your alternative? Let them print whatever they want? Let her father keep selling stories without consequence?"

"We're suggesting that discretion might serve better than confrontation."

Meghan felt the familiar frustration rise. "Discretion for who? Because it's not serving me. It's serving an institution that doesn't want complications."

The silence that followed felt heavy. The communications staff exchanged glances. The older one spoke carefully. "We're not trying to silence you. We're trying to protect the family."

"By sacrificing me."

"That's not what we're suggesting."

"Then what are you suggesting? Specifically. Because from where I'm sitting, you're asking me to absorb another attack without defending myself."

No answer came that satisfied. They left the meeting with the case proceeding, the palace position clear. They wouldn't support it, wouldn't endorse it, would maintain careful distance while Meghan fought alone. She'd known this was coming. It still hurt.

The *Mail*'s decision to publish the letter was prompted by something that had happened weeks earlier. In February 2019, People magazine ran a cover story featuring anonymous friends defending Meghan. Five women spoke without names, describing her kindness, her work ethic, her devastation at her father's betrayal. The article was meant to counter the relentless negative coverage. Instead, it became ammunition.

The *Mail* argued that Meghan had orchestrated the People article, that she'd authorised friends to speak on her behalf, that this constituted a media campaign that made her expectation of privacy hypocritical. What emerged later, during the lawsuit, was more complicated. Jason Knauf had helped draft talking points for the friends. He'd been involved in the media strategy. And he would testify about this involvement in court, a former employee's evidence undermining his former employer's case.

The lawsuit was filed in October 2019. The *Mail on Sunday* immediately went on the offensive, arguing that Meghan had cooperated with the authors of *Finding Freedom*, that the letter wasn't private because she'd known her father might share it, that she was using the courts to control her public image. Jason Knauf's witness statement provided ammunition for their defence. He'd kept texts, emails, communications showing Meghan had been involved in the book despite public denials, that she'd discussed her father's behaviour with palace staff, that palace communications had been more strategic than they'd publicly acknowledged.

The texts were damaging primarily because they revealed Meghan operating within the system the same way everyone else did. Managing narratives. Providing information to friendly journalists. Trying to control stories. The palace did this constantly. Every royal did. But when Meghan did it, it was presented as evidence of manipulation, calculation, dishonesty.

Knauf's testimony would become a central issue in the appeal. The *Mail* argued he'd provided evidence of contradictions in Meghan's case. Her lawyers argued his testimony was selective, taken out of context, designed to support the institution's interests rather than establish truth. The judges would ultimately side with Meghan on the core copyright issues. But Knauf's involvement left scars that went beyond legal outcomes.

"He kept everything," Harry said, reading through the disclosed materials. "Every text and email. Like he was building a file."

"That's what they do," Meghan replied, her voice flat. "They all do. Everyone who works there. They're documenting you constantly, building evidence in case they need it later. We just didn't know we were being surveilled by our own staff."

Knauf's testimony was devastating not because it proved wrongdoing but because it complicated the narrative. Meghan had to apologise to the court for not disclosing her communications with Knauf earlier. The victory, when it came, was shadowed by the messiness of the process, by the spectacle of a former employee providing evidence against someone he'd once worked to protect. The press framed her as a difficult American princess suing a newspaper for doing its job.

Harry watched her read the coverage, saw the toll it took. "We don't have to do this," he said one evening. "We can drop it."

"No. This is mine. I'm not giving them this too."

"Even if it costs everything?"

She looked at him, saw the fear beneath the question. He was asking if she understood how far the institution would let her fall, how little protection they'd offer. She understood perfectly. "Even then."

The case moved slowly through 2019 and 2020, buried in legal motions and procedural delays. Meanwhile, life continued its relentless forward motion. The Africa documentary aired, their vulnerability turned into ammunition. Staff departure stories continued. The walls kept closing in. Then they left for Canada in December 2019, returning to London in January 2020 to face what would become Megxit. Through it all, the lawsuit ground forward.

The legal victory came on a Friday in February 2021, more than a year after they'd left Britain. Meghan was in the kitchen of their California home when Harry called her name from his office, his voice carrying a tone she couldn't immediately identify. Not quite panic or joy. Something between relief and exhaustion.

She found him staring at his laptop screen, phone in hand, reading something that made his shoulders drop in a way they hadn't in months.

"We won," he said simply.

The High Court had ruled in Meghan's favour. The *Mail on Sunday* had breached her privacy by publishing portions of the letter to her father. The judge's language was unequivocal, clinical in its clarity. The publication was unlawful. Her expectation of privacy was reasonable. The defence arguments were rejected. Meghan read the judgment twice, looking for caveats, for ways it could be twisted, for loopholes that would turn victory into something hollow. But the words stayed clear.

"We won," she repeated, testing the feeling as the words formed on her lips.

Harry stood, pulled her into his arms. They held each other in his office, surrounded by papers and legal documents and the accumulated debris of months spent fighting an institution that had unlimited resources and no deadline. The victory felt significant and somehow insufficient at once. Yes, the court had confirmed what she'd always known, that her privacy mattered, that stealing her words was theft. But the damage had been done years ago. The letter had been published, dissected, misrepresented. Winning now couldn't unpublish it.

Still, it was something. A line drawn. A refusal to stay silent just because challenging power was exhausting.

The legal team called an hour later to discuss next steps, appeals, costs. The *Mail* would fight the decision, drag it out, make victory as expensive as possible. They always did. That was how these battles worked. Institutions with deep pockets could afford to lose slowly, to bleed opponents through attrition even when the law was clear.

The press coverage of the judgment split predictably. Some outlets acknowledged the ruling's significance, reported it straightforwardly. Others framed it as Meghan being litigious, difficult, overly sensitive to criticism.

"Does it feel like winning?" Doria asked when Meghan called to tell her. Meghan thought about the question.

"It feels like being believed. By someone with power to say it matters."

"That's something."

"It is. But it doesn't change what they took from me."

"No," Doria agreed quietly. "It doesn't."

"Queen's fury as Harry and Meghan say: We quit"
Daily Mail, 9 January 2020

9

'Megxit'

The conversations about alternatives had been ongoing for over a year. Every proposed compromise met the same response. The leak came on 7 January, before they'd had a chance to present anything formally. Meghan woke to her phone buzzing incessantly, messages flooding in from friends and publicists and people she barely knew. She picked it up, still half asleep, and saw the headline dominating every news site, "Harry and Meghan to Step Back from Royal Duties."

The story was everywhere. Details of their plan, partially accurate but twisted, presented as fait accompli rather than proposal. Someone had leaked it. Someone who wanted to force their hand, to control how the story broke, to ensure the palace narrative came first.

Harry was already downstairs on the phone, his voice low and furious. Meghan walked down to find him pacing the kitchen, still in pyjamas, one hand pressed against his forehead. He looked up when she entered, and she saw something in his face she'd never seen before. Not just anger. Defeat.

"They leaked it," he said flatly.

"Who?"

"Does it matter? It's out there. We've lost control before we even started."

She sat down at the table, pulled her knees up to her chest. Outside, security was already dealing with photographers who'd appeared at the gate within minutes of the story breaking. The machinery had activated, the feeding frenzy begun. Their carefully planned proposal, meant to be presented privately first, was now public spectacle.

"What do we do?" she asked.

He stopped pacing, looked at her. "We put out our statement. Now. Before they define it for us."

They spent the next two hours writing and rewriting, trying to capture what they wanted in language that couldn't be twisted. A new working model. Financial independence. Geographic flexibility. Continued service to the Queen. They genuinely believed it could work, that the institution would see the logic of it, that compromise was possible.

The statement went live at noon. The world exploded.

The press reaction was immediate and vicious. Headlines called it abdication, betrayal, a dereliction of duty. Commentators who'd never met them declared their marriage doomed, their motivations selfish, their character flawed. Meghan sat on the sofa reading coverage on her phone, each article worse than the last, until Harry gently took the phone from her hands.

"Don't," he said. "It won't help."

"They're destroying us."

"They were always going to."

The palace issued a brief statement that evening. "Discussions with the Duke and Duchess of Sussex are at an early stage. We understand their desire to take a different approach but these are complicated issues that will take time to work through."

Early stage. As if they hadn't been trying to have this conversation for months. As if the institution hadn't ignored every attempt at dialogue until forced to respond publicly.

William called that night. The conversation was brief, strained, ended badly. Harry came back into the room looking gutted.

"He's angry," Harry said quietly.

Meghan didn't ask for details. She could imagine well enough. The heir to the throne, watching his brother walk away, feeling abandoned or betrayed or whatever mix of emotions came with watching someone choose freedom over duty.

The summons to Sandringham came two days later. A meeting, just the family, to discuss next steps. Harry drove up alone. Meghan had wanted to join by phone, to participate in decisions that would determine her future, but the request was denied. She stayed at Frogmore with Archie, excluded from the room where her fate was being decided, aware that the conversation was entirely about her without including her.

He returned late that night, exhausted and hollow. She made tea while he sat at the kitchen table, silent. When he finally spoke, his voice was flat.

"They said no."

William had been particularly firm. "I've put my arm around my brother all our lives," he'd reportedly told the room. "I can't do that any more." The words would be reported later, the finality of them, the sense of a relationship reaching its breaking point. Harry had gone to Sandringham hoping for compromise. He'd found ultimatum.

"No to what?"

"All of it. Half in, half out. Keeping some patronages. Earning our own income. They said it's not possible. Either we're working royals or we're not."

"So we're out completely."

"Yes."

She absorbed this. They'd asked for compromise. The institution had responded with ultimatum. All or nothing. Stay within the machine or leave entirely. No middle ground.

"And security?" she asked. "For Archie?"

Harry replied through half-gritted teeth.

"That's being reviewed."

"Reviewed. What does that mean?"

"It means they're considering removing it."

She thought about the threats. The letters that had arrived at the palace, some specific and detailed, describing violence in language that made security professionals take them seriously. The online posts calling for her death, her son's death, celebrating when violence was threatened. The far-right groups who'd adopted her as a target, posting her photo alongside threats in forums monitored by counterterrorism officials. The palace's own security assessments had concluded she faced credible danger. Met Police had arrested several individuals for making threats. And now, because she and Harry had chosen to leave, that protection would be withdrawn.

A chill moved through her.

"They can't do that."

"They can. They will."

She thought about Prince Andrew, credibly accused of sexual assault by multiple women. The institution had rallied around him. Paid for his legal defence. Allowed him to settle the case quietly. He'd kept his security, and his titles, for years, and his place in the family, albeit diminished.

Her son would lose his protection because his parents had stepped back from royal duties.

Andrew still lived with his ex-wife Sarah Ferguson at Royal Lodge, despite her own history of scandals, cash-for-access controversies, and associations that would eventually include the Epstein network. The family tolerated it. Fergie attended some family events, maintained relationships with her daughters who remained working royals. The institution could forgive, could accommodate, could allow people to remain in the fold when it chose to.

She stood and walked to the window. Security vehicles sat in the drive, officers visible in the darkness. How long would they stay? What happened when they left?

"So what now?" she asked.

"We accept their terms. We give up the titles, the funding, the office. We become private citizens. And we figure out how to stay safe without them."

She turned to face him. "Are you sure? Really sure? Because this is it. Once we do this, we can't take it back."

"I'm sure. Are you?"

She thought about staying. About returning to royal duties, about continuing to absorb attacks while the institution stood silent, about raising Archie in an environment that had shown no willingness to protect them.

"Yes," she said. "I'm sure."

They made the decision formal on 18 January. A statement released jointly with the palace, carefully worded to sound mutual when it felt anything but. Harry and Meghan would step back from royal duties. They would no longer use their HRH titles. They would repay Frogmore Cottage renovations. They would retain private patronages but relinquish royal ones. The review period would end in March 2020, with final decisions made then.

Reading it felt surreal. Their lives reduced to bullet points, their future negotiated by lawyers and palace officials.

They had six weeks to complete their remaining engagements. Six weeks to say goodbye to organisations they'd worked with, to staff who'd supported them, to the life they'd tried so hard to make work.

The first event was a visit to Canada House, thanking them for the hospitality during their December stay. They smiled, shook hands, spoke warmly about their time in British Columbia. The event felt both ordinary and weighted, a normal royal engagement that everyone knew was counting down to an ending.

In private, they were packing. Deciding what to take, what to leave, what mattered enough to ship across an ocean. Meghan walked through Frogmore Cottage's rooms, touching walls they'd decorated, remembering the hope they'd felt moving in. The nursery where Archie had spent his first months. The kitchen where they'd cooked meals together. The garden where they'd planned a future that now belonged to someone else.

On 1 February, they attended a charity event together. The photographers were relentless, shouting questions about whether they were having second thoughts, whether they missed the family, whether Meghan was taking Harry away. They ignored all of it, kept walking, kept smiling, maintained composure even as the questions felt designed to provoke.

That night, Meghan sat in the bath, letting hot water soothe muscles tight from constant tension. Harry came in, sat on the edge of the tub.

"You okay?" he asked.

"I'm angry. At them for making this so hard. At the press for being vicious. At myself for caring what any of them think."

"You're allowed to be angry."

"I thought leaving would feel like relief. It just feels like grief."

He reached down and held her hand. "It's both. We're losing things that mattered. But we're also choosing ourselves. That's not nothing."

She squeezed his hand, let tears come that she'd been holding back for weeks. Not sad tears. Just release. The kind of crying when something breaches after being held too tight for too long.

The Endeavour Fund Awards came on 5 March. A celebration of wounded veterans, a cause Harry had championed for years. He gave a speech, his voice steady but emotion visible in his eyes. Meghan sat in the audience wearing blue, watching him, recognising what they were walking away from. Not just titles and duties, but work that had genuine impact, connections that had genuine meaning.

After the event, veterans came up to thank him, to shake his hand, to tell him what his support had meant. Harry absorbed it quietly, gracefully, and Meghan saw him filing these moments away, reminders that his worth wasn't tied to his title.

The Mountbatten Festival of Music was harder. Military dress, ceremony, tradition. Harry in uniform, Meghan in red, both of them acutely aware this might be the last time they attended such an event. The music was beautiful. Other family members were present, polite but distant, the fracture between them visible to anyone paying attention.

They left quickly after, avoiding the reception. In the car, Harry stared out the window, silent. Meghan didn't push. Some grief required space more than conversation.

The Commonwealth Service at Westminster Abbey was set for 9 March. Their final official engagement. The event that would close this chapter of their lives with ceremony and spectacle and millions watching.

They arrived separately from William and Kate, protocol dictating different entrances for working and non-working royals now. When Harry and Meghan walked to their seats, William and Kate were already positioned. The Cambridges did not turn around. Did not acknowledge their arrival. Did not make eye contact. The freeze was visible to everyone watching, cameras capturing the stiff backs, the careful non-looking, the performance of not-seeing that was louder than any greeting could have been.

Meghan and Harry took their seats in the second row, behind working royals, the positioning itself a message about hierarchy and belonging. The abbey was magnificent, music soaring, the ceremony celebrating Commonwealth unity and shared purpose. Two brothers who'd once been inseparable, sitting rows apart, refusing to acknowledge each other's presence. Two sisters-in-law who'd tried to build relationship, now strangers.

During hymns, cameras caught facial expressions. Kate's face was set, carefully neutral, betraying nothing. William's jaw was tight, his posture rigid with controlled emotion. Harry looked exhausted, holding himself together through sheer will. Meghan kept her composure, the skills learnt from years of being watched serving her one final time.

At the service's conclusion, they processed out. Still no acknowledgment. William and Kate left quickly through their designated exit. Harry and Meghan left through theirs. The physical separation was complete. The fracture captured from multiple angles, photographed by dozens of cameras, broadcast live to millions.

Outside, press were already writing headlines. "Frosty Reception at Final Service." "Brothers' Rift Visible in Abbey." "Sussexes Isolated at Commonwealth Event." The coverage focused on body language, positioning, who spoke to whom, who didn't. The content of the service, the causes being celebrated, the Commonwealth's purpose all disappeared beneath analysis of family dysfunction.

In the car afterwards, Harry stared out the window.

Meghan held his hand.

"That's it then," he said quietly.

"That's it."

They drove back to Frogmore in silence. The cottage was mostly packed, boxes stacked in rooms, spaces emptied of their belongings. It already felt like a place they used to live rather than a home. Archie was with his nanny, protected from the chaos, his routine maintained even as everything around him shifted.

That night, their last night in the UK, Meghan couldn't sleep. She walked through empty rooms, remembering. The early days when everything felt possible. The wedding planning. Bringing Archie home. Late night conversations with Harry about how to make this work. All of it real, all of it now part of a past that felt both very close and impossibly distant.

Harry found her in the nursery, standing by the window, looking out at gardens shrouded in darkness.

"You're going to miss it," he said gently.

"Parts of it. The work. Some of the people. The potential of what it could have been."

"I'm sorry."

She turned to him.

"Don't. You chose me. Us. That's everything."

"I chose us. But I'm still sorry we couldn't make it work."

They kissed and embraced in the empty room, their son asleep down the hall, the future uncertain but chosen.

The engines were already warming when Meghan stepped onto the aircraft. The sky above RAF Northolt was its usual London grey. She'd lived under that sky for years now. Tonight it felt different. Final.

Inside the cabin, the lights were dim. Archie clutched his favourite toy, unaware that this flight would mark an ending. Harry's shoulders carried a tension that never loosened anymore. The door closed behind them with a solid thud. One part ending, one part beginning.

The wheels lifted. A soft jolt. The familiar weightlessness. Beneath them, the lights of London tilted and drifted away.

Harry's voice was low. "You okay?"

She turned to him. "I'm tired," she whispered. "But I'm okay."

She leant her head on his shoulder as the plane climbed through cloud. Far below, London blurred into an indistinct patch of light. A place that had changed her, held her, tested her, and finally pushed her to choose herself.

A long breath out. The first breath of the rest of her life.

Canada received them quietly. No fanfare, no press conference, just arrival and privacy and space to breathe. The house on Vancouver Island was waiting, same place they'd stayed at Christmas, familiar now. They settled back in, established routines, tried to figure out what normal looked like when everything had changed.

Meghan walked on the beach with Archie, watching him toddle through shallow water, delighted by waves and sand. The air smelled like salt and cedar. The sky stretched wide and blue. She could breathe here.

But the peace didn't last. Within days, the press found them again. Photographers with long lenses positioned across the water. Drone footage of the property. The UK tabloids were relentless even across an ocean.

Harry grew increasingly protective, frustrated by the intrusion. One night, after another round of invasive photos appeared online, he threw his phone across the room.

"We can't even walk on our own beach," he said.

"I know."

"This is exactly what we left to escape," he fumed. "And they followed us here."

She didn't have an answer. Just sat with him while he calmed down, while the anger settled into the familiar exhaustion.

By late March, COVID was changing everything. Borders closing, flights grounded, the world entering lockdown. They were stuck in Canada, cut off from family, from England, from any possibility of return even if they'd wanted it. And then security was withdrawn. The Metropolitan Police protection that had been under review was now officially removed. Harry's family, his institution, had decided that protecting his wife and infant son was no longer their responsibility.

A call came from someone unexpected. Tyler Perry, the actor and filmmaker, had never met them in person but had been moved by what he'd watched unfold. He offered them his house in Los Angeles, fully staffed and secured. He offered to pay for private security. A stranger, a black American who understood something about what Meghan was facing, providing protection the monarchy had refused.

In late March, they made the decision to move to Los Angeles, flying privately to the house of a man they'd never met, accepting help from outside because nothing was coming from within. Closer to Meghan's mother, better security infrastructure, more possibility for the work they both wanted to do. They packed again, said goodbye to the island, flew south into American airspace.

Los Angeles received them differently than Canada had. Photographers found them immediately. Security became a constant concern without palace protection. The threat level hadn't decreased because they'd left Britain. If anything, it had intensified. The same groups targeting her before had expanded their efforts. Death threats posted publicly. Packages sent to addresses they'd briefly stayed at, intercepted by security before reaching them. The Met Police had warned them about specific individuals who'd made detailed threats, who'd attempted to locate their residence, who represented genuine danger.

Harry had the same threat level assessment as working royals. His service in Afghanistan, his public profile, his position in line of succession all contributed to security risk that hadn't changed because his grandmother removed his title. But the palace argued that security was connected to working royal status, not actual threat level.

Private security cost hundreds of thousands annually. Money they had to spend because the institution had withdrawn protection. Tyler Perry's generosity carried them through the first months. Then they had to figure out sustainable solutions, hiring their own team, paying from their own accounts, protecting their family.

They rented a mansion in a gated community, hired private security, began the work of figuring out how to survive financially now that royal funding was gone.

Meghan's mother visited often, bringing food, helping with Archie, providing the steady maternal presence Meghan desperately needed. Doria didn't ask questions about what had happened, didn't push for details. She just showed up, helped where she could, loved her daughter through the transition.

One afternoon, sitting in the garden while Archie napped, Doria said quietly, "You did the right thing."

Meghan looked at her mother. "Did I?"

"Yes. No place is worth losing yourself. Not even a palace."

"I wanted to make it work."

"I know. But some things can't be fixed just by trying harder."

They sat in comfortable silence, the California sun warm on their faces. Meghan felt something loosen slightly, some tight knot of guilt or failure beginning to unwind.

July brought its own devastation. Meghan woke one morning with cramping that felt wrong, different from the ordinary discomforts she'd learned to recognise. She was changing Archie's nappy when the pain sharpened, became something she couldn't ignore. She knew before the bleeding started. Knew in the way women know when their bodies are doing something that can't be stopped.

Harry found her on the bathroom floor, Archie playing nearby, unaware. She couldn't speak yet. Just held onto him while her body expelled what might have been their second child. The grief was immediate and physical and somehow also distant, as if happening to someone else while she watched from outside herself.

They drove to the hospital in silence. COVID protocols meant Harry couldn't come inside with her. She sat in the waiting room alone, other women in similar states of loss or fear, everyone masked and distant. The doctor confirmed what she'd already known. Miscarriage. Early, nothing that could have been prevented, nothing she'd done wrong. These things happened. One in four pregnancies. Common, though rarely discussed.

The physical recovery was straightforward. A few days of bleeding, cramping, her body returning to its previous state as if nothing had happened. The emotional recovery was different. She'd lost pregnancies before, years ago, privately. But this one felt heavier. They'd wanted to give Archie a sibling. They'd been trying. And now this loss, this small death that wouldn't be acknowledged publicly, that would remain private grief processed while everything else continued around them.

She wrote about it later, in November, an essay for the *New York Times* titled "The Losses We Share." The response surprised her. Thousands of women writing to say they'd experienced the same thing, had carried the same silent grief, had needed someone to acknowledge that early loss still hurt. The essay helped some people. But it also generated the predictable criticism. That she was seeking attention. That she was exploiting tragedy. That private grief should remain private, even though making it private was exactly what kept women isolated in their loss.

Harry held her through the worst nights, when grief came in waves that made breathing difficult. They didn't tell many people. Her mother knew. A few close friends. The palace was not informed. Some losses were theirs alone, not to be managed by communications staff or weighed for public relations impact.

By summer's end, they'd settled into new rhythms. Harry worked with charities remotely, maintained connections to causes he cared about. Meghan began exploring production opportunities, thinking about projects she wanted to develop. The miscarriage remained with them, not as constant pain but as presence, as reminder of what they'd lost and what they still had. Archie, healthy and growing. Each other. The possibility, eventually, of trying again. They were building something, slowly, incrementally, without palace infrastructure or royal expectations.

The months that followed moved in the way grief makes time move. Fast on the surface, slow underneath. Archie grew. The garden filled in. Harry worked with charities remotely, maintained connections to causes he cared about. Meghan began exploring production opportunities, thinking about projects she wanted to develop. They spoke to his grandmother occasionally, brief calls that maintained connection without resolving anything. Harry barely spoke to his brother. The rift sat alongside the other losses, the miscarriage, the family they'd left behind, the life they'd tried to build. Some weeks felt like progress. Others felt like treading water in an ocean that kept getting deeper.

By the following summer, something had settled. One evening, they sat on their patio, wine glasses in hand, watching the sun set over Los Angeles. The city spread below them, all light and sprawl, familiar territory for Meghan, foreign landscape for Harry.

"Do you regret it?" she asked.

He was quiet for a long moment. "I regret that it had to come to this. But I don't regret choosing you."

"That's not the same thing."

"No. It's not." He turned to her. "I miss parts of it. The work, mostly. Some of the people. But I don't miss feeling trapped. I don't miss watching you suffer. I don't miss being powerless to protect our family."

"So we're okay?"

"We're alive. We're together. Archie's safe. That's more than okay. That's everything."

She leaned against him, felt his arm come around her shoulders. The exit had cost them more than they'd anticipated. Titles, family relationships, the life they'd tried to build. But it had given them space, freedom, and the chance to breathe.

"I love you," she said.

"I love you too."

They sat as darkness settled over the city, two people who'd walked away from a palace to save themselves, uncertain what came next but certain they'd face it together.

The exit was complete. The future waited.

And for the first time in years, that future belonged entirely to them.

"So who is the Royal racist?"
The Sun, 9 March 2021

10

'The Meghan Problem'

A year passed in California with the strange quality of both healing and holding your breath. Meghan planted a garden at the Montecito house, her hands in soil that felt different from London earth, warmer, looser, willing to grow things. Archie learned to run, his legs sturdy beneath him, his laughter filling rooms that no longer echoed with palace silence. Harry worked on projects that mattered to him without needing approval from offices three time zones away. They built routines. Small, ordinary rhythms that felt revolutionary after years of protocols.

The Montecito house they'd purchased in 2020 cost $14.7 million, nine bedrooms, 16 bathrooms, the kind of California estate that looked modest only by comparison to palaces. Critics pointed to the price tag as evidence of hypocrisy, of preaching about service while living in luxury. Supporters noted that they'd paid for it themselves, that no public funds were involved, that the security costs they now bore privately had once been covered by the institution that had withdrawn protection.

But the noise never stopped. The tabloids found new angles when old ones wore thin. The lawsuits crawled forward through legal systems designed to move slowly. The narratives about them calcified into accepted truth, repeated so often that correction felt futile.

One evening in December 2020, Oprah's name came up. Not for the first time. There had been conversations before, tentative, exploring whether speaking publicly might shift something and give them space to define themselves. But the timing had never felt right. The wounds were too fresh. The anger too close to the surface.

This time felt different. Enough distance had accumulated. Enough perspective had settled. Meghan sat on the sofa with Harry, the fire crackling, Archie finally asleep upstairs after his usual bedtime negotiations. They'd been talking about the christening photo, the one the palace had refused to release publicly despite it being royal tradition. About the security being withdrawn. About the small scars that had accumulated into something harder to forgive than any single large betrayal.

"What if we just said it?" Meghan asked. "What if we stopped protecting a system that never protected us?"

Harry was quiet for a long moment, staring into the fire. "You know what will happen. It'll be nuclear. They'll come at us harder than before."

"They're already coming at us. At least this way, people hear it from us first."

"Once we do this, there's no taking it back. No softening it later. We're drawing a line."

Meghan nodded slowly. "I'm tired of being quiet while other people tell our story wrong."

He turned to look at her, a seriousness in his eyes. "Are you sure? Really sure? Because I'll support whatever you decide, but I need to know you've thought through what it'll cost."

She had.

She'd thought about little else for months.

The cost of speaking versus the cost of silence. The risk of being believed versus the certainty of being erased. "I'm sure."

They called Oprah's team the next morning. The conversation was brief, professional, careful. Oprah had known them for years, had attended their wedding, understood the nuances in ways that made her feel safe. Not safe from criticism, that was impossible, but safe from distortion. She would let them speak in complete sentences. She would ask hard questions without trying to trap them.

The Times published a story on 2 March, five days before the interview was scheduled to air. "Duchess of Sussex Faces Bullying Complaint." Anonymous palace sources claiming Meghan had bullied staff members during her time as working royal. Former communications secretary Jason Knauf had submitted a complaint in 2018, the article stated. Two personal assistants had been driven out. Staff had been reduced to tears by her demands.

The timing was surgical. The palace had sat on Knauf's complaint for over two years. They'd done nothing when it was submitted. They'd said nothing when staff departed. But now, five days before the Oprah interview, suddenly this was urgent news requiring public statement.

Buckingham Palace announced they would investigate the allegations. "We are clearly very concerned about allegations in *The Times* following claims made by former staff," the statement read. "Accordingly our HR team will look into the circumstances outlined in the article. Members of staff involved at the time, including those who have left the Household, will be invited to participate to see if lessons can be learned."

Lessons could be learned. The phrasing was careful, non-committal, but the message was clear. Meghan was the problem. The institution was taking concerns seriously. The investigation would be thorough.

Meghan read the article in bed, Harry beside her, both of them understanding immediately what was happening. The palace inoculating against the interview, releasing damaging stories before she could speak, framing her as difficult and aggressive, giving the media a green light to dismiss whatever she said as vengeful lies from a disgruntled employee.

"They're trying to destroy your credibility before you've even spoken," Harry said.

"Will it work?"

"For some people. The ones who already hate you. But for everyone else..." He trailed off, uncertain.

CBS issued a statement standing by the interview. Oprah gave a brief comment that she'd asked Meghan about the allegations and Meghan had addressed them. But the news cycle was dominated by the bullying story. Staff in tears. Duchess Difficult. The narrative they'd tried to establish years earlier, now given official palace validation through an announced investigation.

The investigation results were never published. The palace completed their review in 2022, then announced the findings would remain private. They'd made changes to HR policies, they said. Learned lessons about supporting staff. But the specific allegations, the evidence, the conclusions? Private. The damage to Meghan's reputation was public. The exoneration, if any existed, stayed hidden.

The date was set. Early March. The details were negotiated with the precision of a treaty. Location, duration, topics. What was off limits, though very little was.

The weeks before filming carried a particular tension. Meghan felt it settle in her shoulders, a physical weight that massage couldn't shift. She wasn't sleeping well. She'd wake at three, four in the morning, her mind cycling through everything she wanted to say, everything she feared saying, everything that would be taken out of context regardless of how carefully she phrased it. Harry found her more than once sitting in the kitchen in the dark, just breathing, trying to convince her body that this was the right choice even when her nervous system screamed warnings.

"Second thoughts?" he asked one night, sliding into the chair beside her.

"Hundredth thoughts," she admitted. "But not second guessing. Just scared."

"Me too."

They sat in the darkness, holding hands across the table, two people about to do something that couldn't be undone.

The preparation was strange. There was no script, no rehearsal, just conversations about what needed to be said and how to say it without losing the thread to emotion. Meghan wasn't good at talking about the worst parts. She'd spent years compressing pain into manageable shapes, filing it away, moving forward because stopping meant drowning.

But Oprah needed more than summary. She needed specifics. Details. The moments that made it real.

One afternoon, practising, Meghan tried to explain what it felt like when the palace refused to correct false stories. Harry sat beside her, listening, and she noticed his expression break. He'd known she was hurting. He'd fought for her, defended her, chosen her. But hearing it articulated, hearing the full weight of what she'd endured, his expression changed.

"We're doing this," he said, unquestioningly.

"We're doing this," she confirmed.

Doria came to stay for a few days during the preparation period. She didn't ask many questions, just made herself useful in the ways mothers do. Cooking meals Meghan was too anxious to eat. Playing with Archie as his parents disappeared into offices. Being present without demanding presence be acknowledged.

One evening, after Archie was in bed, Meghan found her mother in the kitchen washing dishes that could have gone in the dishwasher. She picked up a tea towel, started drying.

"You don't have to do this," Doria said quietly. "The interview. You could still cancel."

"I can't. I need to say it. Out loud. Where people can hear it."

"What if they don't believe you?"

Meghan set down a plate, looked at her mother. "Some won't. But some will. And that's enough."

Doria nodded, scrubbing at a pan that was already clean.

"Your father's going to say something. You know that, right? He always does."

"I know."

"And it'll hurt. Even though you expect it."

"I know that too."

They finished the dishes in silence. Before Doria left the kitchen, she pulled Meghan into a hug that lasted longer than usual. "I'm proud of you, baby. For surviving. For speaking. For still being here."

Meghan held on tight, breathing in her mother's familiar scent, storing up strength for what was coming.

The night before the interview, Meghan laid out three different dress options on the bed. Black. Navy. The black with white embroidery. She stood staring at them, unable to decide, each choice feeling weighted with meaning it shouldn't have. It was just a dress. But it wasn't. Every element would be analysed, interpreted, turned into evidence of some intention she may or may not have had.

Harry came in, looked at the dresses, looked at her face.

"The one with the embroidery," he said. "It's you. Formal but not trying too hard. Honest."

She picked it up, held it against herself in the mirror. "What if I can't do it? What if I get there and I just freeze?"

"Then we'll stop. We'll leave. It's your story. You control how it's told."

"Do I? Because it feels like the story's been out of my control since the day we met."

He came up behind her, his hands on her shoulders, both of them looking at their reflection. "Tomorrow you take it back. That's what this is. Reclaiming your own story."

She wanted to trust that speaking would give her power rather than just more ammunition to be used against her. But she'd learned too well how words could be twisted, how truth could be reframed as manipulation, how the institution and its allies could turn any attempt at honesty into evidence of ulterior motive.

The morning of the interview arrived with California sunshine that felt almost mocking in its cheerfulness. Meghan dressed carefully, the black dress with white embroidery across the shoulders feeling both formal and honest. Her hair stylist worked in near silence, understanding that today wasn't the day for chatter. The makeup artist kept it simple, natural, just enough to look polished on camera without looking armoured.

Harry wore a light suit, open collar, the sort of casual formality that said he was taking this seriously but wasn't performing royalty anymore. They stood together in the bedroom, looking at each other in the mirror, two people about to drop a bomb and waiting to see what the explosion would destroy.

"Last chance to back out," he said, though his tone suggested he knew they wouldn't.

"Not backing out," she replied.

They drove to the location separately, at different times, to avoid any suggestion that they'd coordinated responses. Meghan arrived first, stepping out into the garden where cameras waited, lights already positioned, the chair that would hold her for the next hour positioned just so.

Oprah was already there, warm, steady, wearing white in deliberate contrast to Meghan's black. They embraced briefly, a moment of genuine affection before the performance began.

"How are you?" Oprah asked, her voice low.

"Terrified," Meghan admitted.

"Good. That means it matters."

They took their positions. The crew faded into background noise. Cameras rolled. And Meghan began speaking truths she'd held silent for years.

The questions came gently at first, building slowly towards harder territory. Oprah asked about the wedding, about those first months, about when things started to shift. Meghan answered carefully, trying to be fair, trying to acknowledge complexity while not hiding from reality. But eventually, inevitably, they arrived at the hardest parts.

"There was a point," Oprah said, her voice measured, "where you've said things became unbearable. Can you take me to that moment?"

Meghan's breath caught. The question hung between them. She had known it was coming. "There were many moments. But there was one time, I was sitting in my room at Nottingham Cottage, and I realised I couldn't do another day. Not another week, not another month. Another day felt impossible."

"What did that feel like?"

"Like drowning. Like the walls were closing in. Like no matter how hard I tried to breathe, there wasn't enough air."

Oprah leaned forward slightly. "Were you thinking of harming yourself?"

The space between the question and Meghan's answer felt enormous, though it was only seconds. She heard Harry shift somewhere off camera. Heard the crew go still.

"Yes."

The word hung in the air between them. Simple. Devastating.

"This was clear and real and frightening and constant," she continued, her voice steadier now that the worst part was out. "I just didn't want to be alive anymore. And that was a very clear and real and frightening constant thought."

"And you went to the institution for help?"

"I did. I went to one of the most senior people. I went to Human Resources, and I said I needed to go somewhere to get help. I said I'd never felt this way before, and I needed to go somewhere. And I was told that I couldn't, that it wouldn't be good for the institution."

There was genuine shock in Oprah's expression. "You were denied help?"

"I was told it wouldn't look good. That there would be headlines. That it was better to handle it privately, quietly, without drawing attention."

"But you were suicidal."

"Yes. But apparently that was less important than protecting the institution's image."

The bitterness in her own voice surprised Meghan. She'd tried to keep emotion out of it, to just state facts. But the facts themselves were so stark that stating them plainly felt like accusation.

Oprah paused, letting the moment sit. Then she switched direction slightly. "I want to ask about something else. There's been reporting about concerns within the family about Archie. About conversations about his skin colour."

Meghan felt her body tense. This was the other revelation, the one she'd debated including at all. Harry had relayed the conversations to her, disgusted and angry. But sharing them publicly meant escalating in ways they couldn't take back.

"In those months when I was pregnant," Meghan said slowly, "we had in tandem the conversations of him not being given security or a title, and also concerns and conversations about how dark his skin might be when he was born."

"What?" The word came out of Oprah like reflex, shock overriding polish.

"There were several conversations about it. About what that would mean, what that would look like."

"Who was having these conversations?"

Meghan shook her head slightly. "I think that would be very damaging to them. The family know who said it. And I hope they'll address it with that person privately."

"So there's a person or persons in the royal family who had concerns about how dark Archie's skin would be?"

"Yes. And that was relayed to me from Harry. Those were conversations he had with family members."

Oprah sat back slightly, visibly processing. "I'm trying to understand. When you say concerns about skin colour..."

"Concerns about what that would mean. If Archie's skin was dark. How that would be perceived. What the implications would be."

The words sat heavy in the garden. Meghan knew how they would explode when this aired, the accusations that would follow. But they were true. And she was tired of protecting people who'd never protected her.

Oprah moved carefully through follow-up questions, trying to get clarity without pushing too hard. Then she moved to Kate, to the bridesmaid dress story that had dominated headlines for months.

"The narrative was that you made Kate cry," Oprah said. "But you've said that's not true?"

"No. The reverse happened. She was upset about something, about the flower girl dresses, and it made me cry. It really hurt my feelings."

"So Kate made you cry?"

"Yes. She apologised, sent flowers, she owned it. I don't say that to be disparaging to anyone, because it was a really hard week of the wedding. And she was upset about something. But she owned it and apologised. And I've forgiven her."

"But the story in the press was very different."

"Yes. And I waited for the palace to correct it. Because they could have. They've corrected stories before about other family members. But this one, they said nothing."

"Why do you think that is?"

Meghan chose her words carefully. "I don't know. I can only tell you what happened and how it made me feel. The story was false. It was provably false. And they let it run uncorrected for months. Years."

When Harry joined them, the dynamic shifted slightly. He was angrier than Meghan, less careful, more willing to burn bridges she was still trying not to fully destroy. He spoke about being cut off financially. About security being removed. About his family being trapped inside the same system that had destroyed them, unable to leave because leaving meant losing everything.

"I wouldn't have been able to do this had I not been financially supported by my mother," he said, referencing Diana's inheritance, the money that had given them freedom when the family withdrew funding. "I've got what my mum left me. And without that, we wouldn't have been able to do this."

Oprah pressed him on relationships with family members. He answered honestly, painfully, admitting distance, admitting hurt, but also admitting love. "I love William to bits," he said. "We've been through hell together. But we're on different paths."

The whole thing lasted over three hours, though only 90 minutes would air. When the cameras finally stopped rolling, Meghan felt emptied, wrung out, like she'd left a big part of herself in that garden with Oprah. Harry came to her immediately, his arms wrapping around her without speaking. They stood like that while the crew packed equipment, two people who'd just dropped a bomb and were waiting to see what the explosion would destroy.

The days before the broadcast were strange, suspended time where everything felt both normal and catastrophically not. They took Archie to the park. They cooked dinner. They pretended, mostly successfully, that life was continuing normally. But underneath, the countdown hummed. Five days. Four days. Three.

The palace got advance warning, a brief summary of what was coming. Meghan didn't know exactly what they'd been told, but she could imagine. The conversations happening in private offices, the crisis management mobilising, the careful consideration of how to respond without making things worse.

Harry was restless during that week, unable to settle into anything. He'd start projects and abandon them. Pick up his phone, set it down, pick it up again. Go for runs that lasted longer each day. Meghan recognised the behaviour. He was bracing for impact, trying to burn off anxiety that had nowhere productive to go.

On Thursday, three days before the broadcast, William called. Harry took it in his office, door closed. Meghan heard his voice rise once, then go quiet. When he emerged a few minutes later, his face was carefully blank.

"He's seen the summary," Harry said. "He wanted me to know they're hurt. That this is going to damage the family."

"What did you say?"

"That I'm hurt too. That we're hurt. That maybe if they'd listened when we asked for help, we wouldn't be here."

"How did he respond?"

"He didn't. He just said there would be consequences."

Meghan felt a shiver. Consequences. The word felt like threat and promise at once. "What kind of consequences?"

"He didn't specify. But I can imagine."

They sat in heavy silence as Archie played with blocks on the floor, unaware of the storm building around him.

Friday was worse. The British tabloids had somehow got more details, were running advance stories about the racism revelations, the mental health crisis, the rifts with family. The coverage was framing it before anyone had seen the actual interview, poisoning the well, setting narrative frames that would be hard to shift.

Meghan stopped reading after the third article. Harry physically took her phone away.

"Don't," he said firmly. "Not until after. Reading it now won't help."

"I want to know what they're saying."

"You know what they're saying. The same things they always say. That you're lying, that you're manipulative, that you've turned me against my family. None of it's new."

She knew he was right. But the compulsion to look, to see, to know exactly how she was being characterised felt almost physical.

Saturday, the night before broadcast, they put Archie to bed together, lingering longer than usual over the bedtime routine. Extra stories. Extra songs. The comfort of ordinary ritual before everything changed. After he was asleep, they sat on their patio with wine and silence.

"Last chance to stop it," Meghan said quietly. "We could call *CBS*, tell them not to air it."

"Do you want to?"

She thought about the question honestly. "No. Do you?"

"No. But I wanted to give you the option."

They clinked glasses, a toast to choices that couldn't be unmade. The California night was clear, stars visible despite light pollution, the air carrying the scent of jasmine from the garden.

It felt surreal that this peaceful moment was the calm before a storm they'd deliberately created.

The interview aired on Sunday 7 March 2021, at 8pm American time, the middle of the night in Britain. Meghan and Harry didn't watch. They couldn't. Instead, they put Archie to bed, turned off their phones, and sat together in the living room with wine and silence. Somewhere, millions of people were hearing them speak. Somewhere, the world was forming opinions, taking sides, deciding what it all meant. But in their house, there was just quiet and the small sounds of their son sleeping upstairs.

They turned their phones back on the next morning. The mistake was immediate. Thousands of messages, calls, notifications. The coverage was everywhere, every angle, every interpretation. Some outlets led with the racism revelations. Others with the mental health crisis. Still others focused on the rift with the royal family, on palace response, on what this meant for the monarchy's future.

The headlines were brutal in their variety.

"Meghan's Bombshell Interview Rocks Palace."

"Prince Harry Accuses Family of Trapping."

"Queen 'Saddened' by Claims."

CNN led with the racism revelations, bringing in royal experts and civil rights leaders to contextualise. "Meghan Markle Details Conversations About Archie's Skin Colour" read the banner beneath footage of her in the garden with Oprah. The American coverage was largely sympathetic, framing it as institutional failure, as a biracial woman failed by a predominantly white establishment.

British coverage split more dramatically. *The Guardian* and *The Independent* ran thoughtful pieces about structural racism, about the monarchy's failure to modernise. But the tabloids went savage.

The *Daily Mail* devoted six pages to "Meghan's Lies Exposed," citing unnamed palace sources refuting specific claims, questioning her mental health, suggesting she'd manipulated Harry into believing a false narrative.

The Andrew comparison emerged in coverage, though not always explicitly. Several commentators noted that the institution had spent millions defending a prince accused of sexual assault while withdrawing security from a prince's wife being threatened with violence. The palace declined to comment on the discrepancy.

Piers Morgan went on *Good Morning Britain* and said he didn't believe a word she'd said. "I don't believe she was suicidal," he announced to millions of breakfast television viewers. "I don't believe those conversations about Archie happened the way she's describing. This is a calculated attack on the royal family by someone who's always been good at playing the victim."

His comments sparked their own controversy. Nearly 60,000 complaints to Ofcom in the first 24 hours. Mental health charities issuing statements about the danger of dismissing suicidal ideation. Morgan doubled down on Twitter, then tripled down on his show the next day. By Tuesday morning, he'd walked off set after a confrontation with a co-host, then resigned entirely. The first major casualty of the interview's aftermath.

The palace statement came late on Monday, careful and measured. "The whole family is saddened to learn the full extent of how challenging the last few years have been for Harry and Meghan. The issues raised, particularly that of race, are concerning. Whilst some recollections may vary, they are taken very seriously and will be addressed by the family privately."

Whilst some recollections may vary. The phrase had been Kate's insistence. In the crisis meetings that followed the interview, as the palace drafted and redrafted its response, Kate had made her position clear. "History will judge this statement," she reportedly said, "and unless this phrase or a phrase like it is included, everything that they have said will be taken as true." William's aide, Jean-Christophe Gray, crafted the final wording.

On Tuesday morning, Meghan woke to 437 text messages. She didn't read most of them. But she saw names of people who'd been silent before now reaching out. Old colleagues from *Suits*. Friends from university. People she'd worked with on humanitarian trips. The support felt validating but also overwhelming. By Tuesday afternoon, viewing figures were released. 17.1 million people had watched in the US. The most-watched entertainment special since the Oscars. Britain wouldn't air it until Monday night on *ITV*, but illegal streams had spread across social media, commentary building before official broadcast.

In the days after the broadcast, Harry gave a brief interview to James Corden, clarifying one point that had consumed speculation. The conversations about Archie's skin colour had not involved the Queen or Prince Philip. "I would never share the full details of that conversation," he said, but he was clear about who it wasn't. The rest of the family remained under suspicion. No one else was explicitly cleared.

Harry's phone rang Tuesday evening. Caller ID showed it was his father. They spoke for 18 minutes. When Harry came back to the living room where Meghan was feeding Archie dinner, his expression was complicated.

"He's angry," Harry said quietly. "But also hurt. He says the racism thing is being misunderstood, that it wasn't meant how it sounded."

"How did it sound to you when it happened?"

"Awful. Like they were worried our son would be too black for the family."

"Then that's what it was."

He nodded slowly. "I told him that. I told him intentions don't change impact. That we'd tried to address this privately and been ignored. That going public was a last resort."

"What did he say?"

"That there are always two sides. That the institution has constraints. That we should have given them more time."

Meghan felt anger rise, hot and immediate. "More time? We gave them years. We tried everything short of disappearing entirely."

"I know. I said that. But I don't think he hears it. I don't think they can hear it."

They sat in heavy silence while Archie smeared sweet potato across his face, oblivious to the chaos surrounding his small existence. Meghan watched her son, felt fierce gratitude that he'd never have to perform happiness while he was dying inside at the same time. Whatever else the interview cost them, at least he'd grow up free of that particular prison.

Weeks turned into months. The interview faded from headlines, replaced by other scandals, other dramas. Life resumed its normal patterns. Archie grew. Meghan worked on projects that mattered to her. Harry continued his advocacy. They built the life they'd said they wanted when they'd left, the life that had seemed impossible from inside palace walls.

But the interview remained, archived, searchable, a permanent record of what they'd endured and how they'd survived it. Sometimes Meghan would think about sitting in that garden with Oprah, saying aloud the things she'd held silent for years. She'd wonder if she'd said too much or not enough, if she'd been fair or too harsh, if the cost had been worth the temporary catharsis.

She never arrived at clean answers. But she knew one thing. Silence had been destroying her. Speaking had been survival.

“Not Heiry Friendly: Prince Harry 'has sidelined anyone
who voiced reservations about Meghan Markle'"
The Sun, 18 June 2019

11

'She's Changed Him'

The Oprah interview aired in March 2021, creating its own firestorm. The legal victory against the *Mail on Sunday* came the month before, confirming what Meghan had known all along. By late 2021, they were learning to exist in the aftermath, building rather than just defending.

Netflix approached in late 2021. A documentary series, a chance to tell their story more fully, more contextually than a single interview could contain. The initial response from Harry and Meghan was caution. They'd just survived one round of public vulnerability. Did they want to do it again? But the offer was different. They'd have creative control. They'd be producing, shaping the narrative, not just sitting for someone's questions.

The conversations about what the documentary would cover stretched over months. Production teams, archival footage, interviews with friends and experts. They wanted it to be more than their story. They wanted context. History. The ways media and monarchy had collided before, the patterns that repeated across generations. Diana's story woven through theirs. The pressure that builds inside systems designed to resist change.

Filming was strange. Cameras in their home, capturing ordinary moments that would become public. Archie playing in the background, carefully kept out of frame. Lilibet, born in June 2021, sleeping in her cot whilst her parents talked about racism and institutional failure and choosing survival over tradition. The juxtaposition felt surreal. This was their life now. Private moments staged for public consumption because public consumption had already claimed them. At least this way, the framing was theirs.

Harry struggled more with the documentary than Meghan did. He'd grown up inside cameras, but always with palace machinery controlling access, managing narrative. This was different. This was him speaking without protocol officers editing his words, without palace approval shaping his message. It felt liberating and terrifying in equal measure.

One afternoon, filming an interview section, he stopped mid-sentence and looked directly at the camera. "I'm scared this will make everything worse. That we're just adding fuel to a fire that's already burning us."

The director kept rolling. "Do you want to stop?"

Harry shook his head slowly. "No. Because staying silent hasn't helped either. At least this is our fire."

The news about Harry's memoir came in stages. First the announcement, brief and professional, that he was writing a book. Then the speculation about what it would contain. Then the reality, as publication approached, that this wouldn't be a gentle reflection. This would be the fullest accounting yet of what it felt like to grow up inside the machine.

Harry wrote in a small office off their bedroom, door closed, hours passing in silence broken only by typing. Meghan left him alone during those sessions, understanding that this was something he needed to do without her watching. The grief he carried was older than their marriage, deeper than any single relationship.

His mother. His childhood. The ways he'd been shaped by trauma and expectation and the particular loneliness of being royal.

Sometimes he'd emerge looking gutted, wrung out, like he'd performed surgery on himself. Other times he looked lighter, unburdened, as if getting words onto pages released something he'd been carrying too long.

One afternoon in early autumn, she brought him tea and found him crying at his desk, laptop open to a section about Diana's funeral. He'd written and deleted the same paragraph six times, trying to capture what it felt like to be twelve years old, walking behind your mother's coffin whilst the world watched, your grief turned into public spectacle.

He was also writing about the days immediately after her death. The palace's cold response, the institution prioritising protocol over grief, the way they'd had to beg for permission to have a public funeral at all. The Queen's initial refusal to return to London, to address the nation, to acknowledge that something unprecedented had happened. The public fury that had finally forced the family to respond.

He was drawing parallels, though he wasn't always explicit about them. The way the institution had failed Diana. The way it was failing Meghan. The patterns that repeated because nothing fundamental ever changed.

"I can't get it right," he said, voice rough. "Every time I try to write it, it comes out either too detached or too emotional. I can't find the balance."

Meghan set down the tea, pulled a chair beside him. "Maybe there isn't a balance. Maybe some things are just both."

"The editor wants me to add more context. Historical background. What was happening politically, why Diana died the way she did. But that's not what I remember. I just remember the coffin. The flowers. The noise of people crying who'd never met her."

"Then write that. Your memory, not the historical record."

He looked at the screen, at the paragraph he'd been wrestling with. "They'll say I'm being manipulative. Using my mother's death for sympathy."

"They'll say that regardless of what you write. So you might as well write the truth."

The truth was complicated. Harry loved his family despite everything. Loved his brother even though their relationship had fractured. Loved his father whilst being angry at his failures. The book couldn't be simple takedown or uncomplicated tribute. It had to hold all the contradictions simultaneously.

He wrote about Afghanistan in clinical detail, the mechanics of combat, the rules of engagement, the kill count that would later become its own controversy. He wrote about drugs with uncomfortable specificity. Cocaine at someone's country house. Mushrooms that made him feel a bin was talking to him. Cannabis that helped him cope. The admissions were strategic in their way, removing the power of future exposures by exposing himself first, but they also revealed the extent of his struggles, the years of self-medication that had preceded therapy. He wrote about drug use with the honesty of someone who'd stopped caring about protecting his image.

He wrote about Camilla with particular care. Not just his complicated feelings toward the woman who'd been part of his parents' marriage collapse, but the mechanics of how her rehabilitation had worked. The strategic briefings. The careful PR campaign. The stories planted in sympathetic outlets. The way negative coverage of other family members seemed to coincide with positive coverage of her. He didn't accuse directly. He simply documented the pattern. Readers could draw their own conclusions.

The sections about Camilla's office were among the most legally scrutinised. Her team had spent years cultivating press relationships, trading information, managing her image from villain to acceptable to beloved Queen Consort. Harry wrote about conversations, about things said in confidence, about the briefing wars that happened behind palace walls while everyone smiled for cameras.

His editor pushed back on some details. Too specific. Too likely to cause diplomatic crisis. Harry reluctantly softened a few passages. But the substance remained. Camilla had needed good press to become acceptable. That good press had sometimes come at other people's expense. He wrote about the Nazi costume incident that had haunted him for years, revealing that William and Kate had laughed when he'd tried it on, that they'd encouraged him to wear it over a pilot uniform. The blame, when the photograph emerged, had fallen on Harry alone. The laughter had been shared.

And he wrote about William. The brother who'd been his closest friend, his protector, his partner in processing grief. The physical altercation that had happened at Nottingham Cottage, when an argument about Meghan had escalated until William grabbed him by the collar, knocked him backwards, and sent him crashing to the floor onto a dog bowl that shattered beneath him. Harry had sat on the floor, stunned, while William stood over him, then left. Their father had tried to mediate afterwards, but something had broken that couldn't be reassembled. The distance between them had grown into a chasm neither seemed able to bridge.

That section took longest. Meghan would hear him on the phone with his editor, debating language, tone, whether to include specific details or let them remain private. He wanted to be honest without being cruel. Fair without minimising his own pain.

"I don't want to hurt him more than I already have," Harry said one evening, reading through the William sections for the tenth time. "But I also can't lie about what happened. About how it felt to have him physically attack me, then act like I was crazy for being upset about it."

"You're allowed to tell your story. Even when it involves other people."

"But what if telling my story makes reconciliation impossible?"

Meghan didn't have an answer. That was the risk. Speaking truth often was. You could stay silent and preserve the possibility of connection, or you could speak and accept that some relationships couldn't survive honesty.

In March 2022, William and Kate toured the Caribbean. Three countries in eight days, marking the Queen's Platinum Jubilee, reinforcing Commonwealth ties. The tour was meant to demonstrate the monarchy's continued relevance, its ability to represent Britain abroad, its modern face.

It became a public relations catastrophe.

Photographs appeared of William and Kate shaking hands with Jamaican children through chain-link fence, the optics immediately compared to colonial imagery, to viewing subjects through barriers, to treating people as exhibitions rather than equals. Protests erupted at multiple stops. Activists demanding reparations for slavery. Groups calling for Jamaica to remove the British monarch as head of state. The smiling, waving, carefully choreographed appearances colliding with growing anger at what the monarchy represented.

Kate wore clothes that drew immediate comparison to colonial-era fashion. Green dress, white gloves, the aesthetic of empire. Jamaican officials pointedly declined to greet them with the warmth protocol suggested. The Prime Minister stated publicly that Jamaica was "moving on" and would soon become a republic. The Bahamas government issued statements about addressing "the wrongs of the past."

British media tried to frame it as successful despite challenges. But the images told different stories. William and Kate in an open-top Land Rover, reviewing troops, the visual indistinguishable from colonial administrators inspecting subjects. The Duke and Duchess dancing with locals in carefully staged photo opportunities that felt performative rather than genuine.

Harry called William afterwards. Brief, strained, the first time they'd spoken in months. William sounded defensive, exhausted, unwilling to admit the tour had been disaster.

"The media made it look worse than it was," William said.

"The media showed what happened. People protesting. Governments calling for independence. You and Catherine behind fences like you were visiting a zoo."

"We were doing our duty. Representing the Queen."

"That's the problem. The duty requires you to pretend empire never happened. People remember, William. They're not going to keep pretending with you."

William ended the call shortly after. The tour's failure accelerated conversations across the Commonwealth. Barbados had already become a republic in November 2021, removing the Queen as head of state in a dignified ceremony that demonstrated you could respect history without remaining bound to it. Jamaica began formal proceedings toward the same end. Belize, the Bahamas, others followed.

The Platinum Jubilee brought them back to London in June 2022, 70 years since Elizabeth II's accession. Celebrations planned across the UK, the Commonwealth, beyond. The invitation extended to Harry and Meghan, though not as working royals. They could attend, but not on the balcony. Not in the official photographs. Present but not part of the performance.

They brought both children. Archie, now three, understood the trip as visiting family in a faraway place. Lilibet, nearly one, understood nothing except that routines had changed and travel was exhausting.

The meeting happened at Windsor, private, family only. The Queen seeing her great-granddaughter for the first time. The only time, though nobody knew that then. Meghan dressed Lilibet in something soft and simple, nothing too formal, just a baby meeting her great-grandmother. Harry held her as they entered, then set her down on the carpet.

The Queen was smaller than Meghan remembered. Frailer. But her eyes were sharp, taking everything in. She smiled at Lilibet with genuine warmth, the kind of smile that suggested she'd always loved children even if protocol usually kept them at a distance.

"She has your hair," the Queen said to Harry.

"She has her mother's spirit," he replied.

They stayed perhaps half-an-hour. Long enough for photographs that would remain private. Long enough for Lilibet to warm to this small elderly woman who spoke softly and held her hand gently. Too brief to build real connection. Just long enough to establish that this meeting had happened, that the Queen had known both her great-grandchildren, that geography and choice hadn't completely severed all ties.

Afterwards, walking back through Windsor's corridors, Meghan felt the weight of it. This might be the last time. The Queen was 96, visibly declining, the fragility evident despite her composure. This brief meeting might be all Lilibet would ever have of her great-grandmother. A few minutes on a carpet in Windsor, captured in photographs that would remain private, filed away as evidence of a relationship that had barely existed.

"She seemed happy to meet her," Harry said quietly.

"She did."

"But it wasn't enough. None of this is enough."

Meghan didn't disagree.

They'd travelled 5,000 miles for 30 minutes of family contact that should have been ordinary. Should have been weekends and holidays and gradual relationship building. Instead, it was this. A formal visit. Cameras kept out but protocol kept in.

The Jubilee celebrations continued around them. The pageantry, the crowds, the carefully choreographed events that marked seven decades of Elizabeth II's reign. Harry and Meghan attended the Service of Thanksgiving at St Paul's Cathedral, sitting in the second row, away from working royals. The congregation rose when they entered. Some people booed. Some people cheered. The division was audible, visible, impossible to ignore.

The balcony appearance was for working royals only. This had been made clear in advance. Harry and Meghan watched from inside, away from cameras, as the family gathered on that famous balcony for photographs that would define the Jubilee coverage. The Queen, Charles, Camilla, William, Kate, their children. The line of succession. The institution's future.

"We used to be up there," Harry said quietly, watching through a window.

"I know."

"It was terrible. The performance of it. The smiling on command. But at least we belonged."

"We belong with each other. That's enough."

He turned from the window. "Is it?"

She took his hand. "It has to be."

They left before the weekend ended. The children needed routine. California needed them more than London did. They'd made their appearance, fulfilled the obligation, proved they could be civil even when the institution continued making clear they weren't truly welcome.

Flying home, Lilibet asleep in Meghan's arms, Archie dozing against Harry's shoulder, Meghan thought about the meeting.

Her daughter had met the Queen. That was something. At least Lilibet had been seen, acknowledged, included in however limited a way.

"Do you think she'll remember?" Harry asked, looking at their daughter.

"Lilibet? No. She's too young."

"Then what was the point?"

"The point is we tried. We showed up. We gave them the chance. What they do with that chance is their choice, not ours."

He nodded slowly, accepting the logic, even if it didn't ease the sadness.

The call came on 8 September 2022. Harry was in London, preparing for a charity event. Meghan was meant to join him. His grandmother was failing. The family was gathering at Balmoral. He needed to come immediately.

He booked the first available flight to Scotland, and texted Meghan to stay in California with the children. The journey felt endless. Checking his phone compulsively. No updates. Just the growing certainty that he wouldn't arrive in time.

The plane landed at Aberdeen. His phone showed a text from his father. "Call me when you land." He knew before dialling. His grandmother, the Queen, was dead. She'd died hours ago, while he was in the air, unreachable. The *BBC* had announced it before he'd been told. He'd learned his grandmother was dying the same way the public had.

The days that followed blurred together. Meghan flew to join him. They stayed at Frogmore, the cottage they'd left two years earlier, now strange and unfamiliar. The family gathered for ceremonies, for vigils, for the lying in state that drew hundreds of thousands to queue for hours.

The palace suggested a joint appearance. William and Kate, Harry and Meghan, together at Windsor to view floral tributes.

The four of them walked the grounds where so much had fractured, cameras tracking every gesture, every space between them. They smiled politely. They split up quickly. The performance of unity lasted exactly as long as the cameras required.

Harry wanted to wear his military uniform for the vigil. He'd served ten years, deployed twice to Afghanistan, earned the right to the uniform by any reasonable standard. But he was no longer a working royal. The uniform was denied. Public outcry forced a reversal. He could wear it for the vigil, the palace announced.

The funeral itself was grand, meticulous, steeped in tradition accumulated over centuries. Harry and Meghan sat in the second row at Westminster Abbey, close enough to see everything, far enough to mark their distance from the core family. Meghan wore black, a veiled hat, pearl earrings the Queen had given her years ago when things had still felt possible.

After the service, the procession to Windsor. The committal service at St George's Chapel, the same space where they'd married four years earlier. Then the private burial, family only, photographers finally excluded. Harry stood with his father and brother, the three of them together but not together, grief complicated by everything between them.

They flew back to California two days after the funeral. Archie and Lilibet had questions about where they'd been, why Great-Granny wasn't coming to visit anymore. Harry tried to explain death to children too young to grasp permanence, his own grief visible beneath the careful age-appropriate language.

"She loved you both very much," he told them. "Even though we didn't see her often, she thought about you all the time."

Lilibet, at 15 months, seemed to accept this without deep understanding. Archie, nearly four, had more questions. Why couldn't they visit her? Why did they live so far away? Why didn't the family all live together like his friends' families?

Harry answered as honestly as he could without burdening them with adult complexity. But the questions sat heavy. His children would grow up without really knowing their paternal great-grandmother, their grandfather, their uncle. Distance measured in oceans and choices and institutional failures that couldn't be explained to a preschooler.

"Do you think she understood?" Meghan asked one night, after the children were asleep, after they'd returned to their California routine. "Why we left?"

Harry was quiet for a long time. "I think she understood duty. I don't know if she understood choosing yourself over duty. That wasn't her framework."

"Do you regret not being able to say goodbye properly?"

"I regret a lot of things. But not leaving. Never leaving."

The Queen's death closed a chapter. Elizabeth II had reigned for 70 years, longer than most people alive could remember. She'd been constant, present, the face on currency and stamps and the embodiment of an institution that predated her and would continue after her. Her passing felt seismic in ways that went beyond personal grief.

For Harry, it meant his father was now King. The same father who'd cut him off financially, who'd stopped taking his calls, who seemed unable to understand why his son had chosen his wife and children over royal duty.

For Meghan, it meant the loss of the one person in that family who'd seemed to genuinely wish them well. The Queen had been formal, distant, bound by protocol and institutional loyalty. But she'd also been kind in her way, had welcomed Meghan with warmth those first meetings, had given her pearl earrings and included her in things. The fact that institutional pressure had eventually overwhelmed personal kindness didn't erase the kindness that had existed.

They grieved separately and together. Harry for the grandmother he'd loved, for the relationship that had survived everything until geography and institutional politics made it impossible. Meghan for the loss of the last thread connecting Harry to a family that had never quite accepted her but that she'd hoped, naively perhaps, might eventually soften.

Harry kept writing. Through autumn into winter, the manuscript growing, taking shape. Some days he'd write thousands of words, the memories flowing faster than he could type. Other days he'd stare at blank screen for hours, paralysed by the weight of what he was attempting.

Meghan read sections as he finished them. To bear witness. To be present whilst he excavated decades of grief and anger and love that had nowhere else to go. Some sections made her cry. Others made her furious at systems that had damaged him so fundamentally.

"Do you think people will understand?" he asked one night, after finishing a particularly difficult chapter about his relationship with Charles.

"Some will. Others won't. But you're not writing for everyone. You're writing for people who need to hear that even princes can be fucked up by their families. That privilege doesn't protect you from pain."

He nodded slowly. "And for our kids. So when they're older, when they ask questions, there's a record. My version. Not what the tabloids said or what the history books will write."

That became the anchor. Not public reception, sales figures or critical acclaim. Just leaving a record. His truth, documented, permanent.

Whatever happened after publication, at least he'd said it.

The final manuscript was 416 pages. Harry submitted it in November, too late to take anything back, too committed to second-guess. They had three months until publication. Three months to brace for the explosion they both knew was coming.

The documentary aired in December 2022, six weeks before the book. Six episodes, each building on the last, weaving their personal story through larger contexts of media, race, institutional power. Friends spoke on their behalf. Experts provided historical context. Archival footage showed patterns repeating across generations.

The first three episodes focused on their courtship, the early pressures, the media scrutiny that intensified so quickly. The second three went darker. The racism. The mental health crisis. The decision to leave. The aftermath. It was comprehensive in ways that made the Oprah interview look like a brief introduction.

The palace stayed silent for days, then issued another brief statement expressing disappointment, defending the institution without addressing specific claims.

"We could show them video footage and they'd call it deepfake," Harry said one night, scrolling through comments that accused them of fabricating everything.

"So why did we do it?" Meghan asked, not challenging but genuinely wondering.

"For the people it does reach. For the ones who needed to hear someone say what they've experienced. For our kids, so when they're older they'll know we told the truth."

The book was titled *Spare*. A reference to his position in the family, the expendable one, the insurance policy for the heir. The title alone sparked debate before anyone had read a word. Some thought it was clever, cutting. Others thought it was bitter, self-pitying. Harry didn't defend it. The title meant what it meant.

Publication was set for January 2023. The timing was deliberate. Far enough from the documentary to be separate, close enough to feel like part of the same conversation. As the date approached, the press got hold of advance copies. Spanish editions leaked early. Excerpts appeared in tabloids days before the official release, pulled out of context, sensationalised, twisted into the most inflammatory possible interpretations.

Harry fought over Afghanistan. Harry and William's physical altercation. Harry's drug use. Harry's kill count. Each revelation stripped of nuance, presented as scandal, weaponised before readers could encounter the actual text with its actual context.

The night before publication, Meghan found Harry standing in Lilibet's room, watching her sleep, his expression unreadable. She came to stand beside him, her hand finding his.

"Having second thoughts?" she asked quietly.

He didn't answer immediately. Just watched their daughter breathe, the gentle rise and fall of her chest under the blanket. "I keep thinking about what this means for them. When they're old enough to read it. To understand what their father went through. What their mother went through."

She heard what he wasn't saying. That speaking might destroy what little remained of his relationships with William, with Charles, with the family that had raised him even as it damaged him. That honesty might cost more than silence ever had.

"We've tried silence," she said. "It didn't work."

"No. But at least silence left room for maybe. Maybe one day we'd reconcile. Maybe one day they'd understand. This closes that door."

"Does it? Or does it just make the terms clear? That reconciliation requires acknowledging what actually happened, not pretending it didn't."

He didn't answer. Just stood watching their daughter sleep, his thumb moving slowly across Meghan's hand. After a while, he said, "I still love them. That's the part that makes it hard. If I hated them, this would be easier."

"Love doesn't mean silence. Sometimes it means the opposite."

"That's what I keep telling myself."

They stood like that for a long time, two people about to make something irreversible public, hoping it was the right choice but knowing they'd never be certain.

The book sold. Massively. Millions of copies in the first week, numbers that broke records, proved demand, validated the choice to speak. But sales didn't equal understanding. The Camilla revelations generated particular fury from palace allies.

Camilla herself said nothing publicly. Charles released a brief statement expressing sadness about family divisions.

Reviews split predictably. Some praised his honesty, his willingness to name dysfunction without euphemism. Others called it a betrayal, an attack on family, proof that he'd been corrupted by Hollywood and his American wife.

That last bit never stopped stinging Meghan, no matter how often she told herself it didn't matter. The idea that Harry's choices were hers to blame for, that he had no agency, no valid reasons beyond her influence.

The book tour was brief, controlled. A few interviews, carefully selected, with journalists Harry trusted not to sensationalise. He talked about his mother's death, about the trauma of walking behind her coffin at twelve.

He talked about Afghanistan, about service. He talked about his family with a mixture of love and pain that resisted simple categorisation. One interview, the journalist asked if he'd reconciled with William.

"I love my brother. I've said that publicly and I'll keep saying it. But loving someone doesn't mean you can have a relationship with them when the circumstances are toxic. I hope for reconciliation. I've tried. But it requires both people wanting it, and I don't know if we're there yet."

Charles's coronation was announced for May 2023. The invitation arrived by formal post, heavy cream paper with gilt edges, the language ceremonial and distant. The Duke and Duchess of Sussex were invited to attend the coronation of King Charles III. No personal note. No acknowledgment of the years of separation, the public battles, the hurt on all sides. Just protocol, proper and cold.

They discussed it for weeks. Attend and face the scrutiny, the cameras searching their faces for signs of reconciliation or lingering rift. Don't attend and face accusations of petty revenge, of putting their grievances above family obligation. There was no good choice, just variations of difficult.

The decision to have Harry attend alone came after weeks of agonising debate. Both go and Meghan becomes the story, overshadowing Charles's day, turning it into referendum on family rifts. Neither go and it's perceived as petty revenge, Harry choosing his wife over his father on the most important day of Charles's life. Harry alone was the compromise that satisfied no one but hurt least.

"I don't want you to go by yourself," Meghan said the night they finalised the decision. They were in bed, the house quiet, both children asleep. "You'll be alone there. Surrounded by family who blame you for everything."

"I'll survive a few hours."

"That's not the same as being okay."

He turned to face her. "If you come, they'll make it about you. Every camera will be on you, every commentator analysing your expression, your dress, where you're seated, whether you look remorseful or defiant. That's not fair to my father. It's his day."

"And you being there alone sends what message? That I don't support him? That we're still fighting?"

"It sends the message that you're home with our daughter on her birthday. It's true, reasonable and what any mother would do."

Lilibet's birthday falling on coronation day had been coincidence or cosmic joke, depending on perspective. The timing gave them cover, a legitimate reason for Meghan's absence that couldn't be easily attacked. But it also meant splitting their family on a day that should have been celebration.

The night before his flight, they had dinner together, just the four of them. Archie asked why Daddy was leaving, why he couldn't come to the party tomorrow. Harry explained about Grandpa becoming King, about important ceremonies, about family obligations that sometimes took you away from the family you'd chosen.

Archie seemed to accept this, the way children do. Lilibet was too young to understand. She just knew Daddy was leaving and she didn't like it.

After the children were in bed, Meghan and Harry sat on their patio, the California night warm around them. "Call me when it's over," she said. "I don't care what time it is here. I want to know you're okay."

"I will."

"And if it's terrible, if they're cruel, you can leave early. You don't have to stay for the whole thing."

"I know."

But they both knew he would stay. Protocol demanded it. Duty demanded it. The same forces that had driven him away still had enough hold to bring him back for this.

He flew out the next morning, early enough that the children were still sleeping. Meghan drove him to the airport, helped him with his bag, held him in the departure area for longer than necessary. "I love you," she said against his shoulder.

"I love you too. Tell Lilibet happy birthday from me."

"She won't remember this one."

"I will."

She watched him go through security, watched him turn once to wave before disappearing into the terminal. Then she drove home alone, back to the house where they'd have a birthday party without him, where she'd spend the day pretending everything was normal whilst watching coverage of an event she'd been half-invited to, half-excluded from.

Harry flew to London, attended the ceremony, sat in the third row rather than the front, between Princess Eugenie and Princess Beatrice rather than beside his brother. He wore morning dress, not military uniform, the distinctions carefully noted by observers tracking every visual signal of his diminished status. He left immediately after the service, skipping the balcony appearance and the family lunch, the whole trip lasting barely 28 hours. He touched down in California in time to celebrate his daughter's second birthday.

The coronation photos would show Harry in the third row, alone, surrounded by family who didn't acknowledge him, his face carefully neutral. Meghan saw the images and felt her chest tighten. He looked isolated in ways that made her grateful she'd stayed home, but also guilty that her absence meant he'd had to face it alone.

When he called that evening, she was in the middle of cutting birthday cake, Lilibet's face covered in frosting. "How was it?" she asked, stepping into the kitchen for privacy.

"Long. Cold. Exactly what I expected."

"Did you talk to William? To your father?"

"Briefly. Surface pleasantries. Nothing real."

She heard the exhaustion in his voice, the weariness of holding composure in hostile territory.

"When do you land?"

"Six hours. I'll be home for breakfast."

"We'll be waiting."

After they hung up, Meghan returned to the party, to her daughter's birthday, to the life they'd chosen. Harry had gone. He'd fulfilled the obligation. Now he could come home.

The lawsuits continued. Phone hacking cases, privacy violations, a seemingly endless parade of legal battles that drained bank accounts and emotional reserves. Harry was determined to hold tabloids accountable for decades of illegal behaviour. Not just for himself, but for everyone who'd been hacked, surveilled, exploited by newspapers that treated laws as suggestions rather than limits.

The legal work was gruelling. Depositions, document reviews, witness statements. Harry spent hours with lawyers, reconstructing years of invasions, proving patterns of behaviour tabloids denied. In December 2023, he won his phone hacking case against Mirror Group Newspapers, the judge ruling that his voicemails had been intercepted and awarding £140,600 in damages. It was the first time a senior royal had given evidence in court in over 130 years. The case against *The Sun*'s publisher continued.

The deposition took place in a conference room in central London, neutral territory chosen by lawyers, windows overlooking the Thames. Meghan had flown in specifically for this, three days away from California, from her children, from the life she'd built. Harry had offered to come, but she'd said no. This was hers to do. The phone hacking lawsuit was hers to fight.

The opposing barrister was a woman in her fifties, expensively dressed, the sort of polished competence that came from decades of defending institutions against individuals. She smiled politely as Meghan entered, as if they were meeting for tea rather than legal combat.

"Your Royal Highness," the barrister said, the title deliberate, a reminder of what Meghan had walked away from.

"Ms Markle is fine," Meghan replied, taking her seat. Her own legal team flanked her, three lawyers who'd spent months preparing her for this. Don't volunteer information. Answer only what's asked. Stay calm regardless of provocation.

The questions started gently. Biographical information, timeline confirmation, establishing basic facts. Then they sharpened. The barrister slid a document across the table, a printout of an article from 2017.

"This article contains details about a private conversation you had with your father. How do you suppose the newspaper obtained that information?"

"My father told them," Meghan said evenly. "He was being paid for stories."

"You're alleging your father sold stories to the press?"

"I'm stating a fact. He admitted it. There are bank records."

"But this particular article…" The barrister tapped the paper. "Your father has stated in his own testimony that this information came from phone messages. Messages you sent him. Messages he received through entirely legal means."

Meghan felt her jaw tighten. "Messages that were private. That he then shared with journalists for money."

"That's not phone hacking though, is it? That's your father choosing to share information you'd given him."

"My father's phone was hacked. The messages were intercepted before he ever saw them. The journalists knew what I'd said before he did."

"Can you prove that?"

Meghan looked at her lawyer, who nodded slightly. They'd been through this. The technical evidence, the phone records, the metadata.

"Yes. Our technical expert has provided detailed analysis."

The barrister smiled, a thin professional thing. "Technical analysis. But you can't know definitively what your father did or didn't share independently, can you? You weren't there."

"I know my father's bank records show payments from three different tabloids. I know articles appeared containing information he couldn't have known unless his phone was compromised. I know the pattern is consistent with dozens of other victims of phone hacking."

"Or it's consistent with a father sharing stories about his daughter becoming a princess. Can you see how those look similar?"

"My father's involvement doesn't negate the hacking," she said carefully. "Even if he also sold stories, that doesn't mean his phone wasn't illegally accessed. Both things can be true."

"Both things can be true," the barrister repeated. "But you're asking the court to award damages based on violations of privacy. Yet you shared much of this information voluntarily with your father. Where's the privacy violation if you chose to tell him these things?"

"The violation is in the interception. In accessing my communications without consent. In publishing private information obtained illegally."

"Information your father may have also provided willingly."

"Which doesn't make the hacking legal."

They went in circles for two hours. The barrister pulling at threads, trying to unravel the case by making everything seem ambiguous, contested, impossible to prove definitively. Meghan answered each question carefully, aware that every word was being recorded, would be analysed, could be used against her later.

By the time they broke for lunch, her head was pounding. She walked to the window, looked out at the Thames moving grey and steady below. London. The city that had nearly destroyed her. She'd returned to fight in its courts, to hold its institutions accountable, and it still felt like drowning.

Her lead lawyer came to stand beside her. "You're doing well. She's trying to provoke you into contradicting yourself. You haven't."

"How much longer?"

"Probably two more hours this afternoon. Then you're done."

She returned to the conference room. The afternoon session was harder. Questions about her relationship with Harry, about whether she'd known what she was getting into, about whether all of this was just revenge for not being protected.

"Isn't it true," the barrister asked, "that you're pursuing this case primarily to damage the newspapers that criticised you?"

Meghan met her eyes steadily. "I'm pursuing this case because my phone was hacked. Because private communications were stolen and published. Because that's illegal. The fact that those newspapers also happened to spend years attacking me doesn't change the illegality of their actions."

"But it does speak to motivation, doesn't it?"

"My motivation is accountability. For crimes committed. Against me and hundreds of others. That's not revenge. That's justice."

The barrister made a note, her expression unchanged. "We'll see what the judge thinks."

One evening in late 2023, they sat on their patio after the children were asleep. The California sky was clear, stars visible despite the light pollution. Meghan had a glass of wine. Harry had tea. They'd been quiet for a while, just existing in each other's presence, when Meghan finally said what she'd been thinking for months.

"I'm tired of fighting."

Harry looked at her, his expression understanding. "Me too."

"But we can't stop, can we? Stopping means they win."

"Maybe. Or maybe stopping means we choose peace over being right."

She thought about that. The machine would keep grinding regardless of whether they engaged with it. The tabloids would keep publishing regardless of lawsuits. The narratives would keep spreading regardless of truth. But maybe Harry was right. Maybe at some point you had to choose your own wellbeing over trying to fix systems designed to resist fixing.

"I don't know how to stop," she admitted. "I've been fighting so long I don't remember what not fighting feels like."

"Neither do I. But maybe we start figuring it out."

They didn't have answers that night. Just questions and exhaustion and the slow recognition that they couldn't keep living in permanent war stance without losing themselves completely.

The legal victories continued to accumulate. Settlements, judgments, rulings in their favour. But each victory felt smaller than anticipated.

By the end of 2023, they'd been in California for nearly four years. Long enough that it felt like home rather than refuge. Long enough that Archie had friends and routines. Long enough that Lilibet had never known any other life. The war was ongoing, but it was no longer consuming them entirely. They'd learned to exist alongside it rather than inside it.

Meghan returned to creative work, producing content that mattered to her, projects that used her voice for more than just defence. Harry's advocacy deepened, focusing on veterans' mental health, on causes he'd championed before the chaos swallowed everything. They were building, not just surviving.

One afternoon, Meghan found Harry playing in the garden with both children. Archie was showing Lilibet how to kick a football. Harry was laughing, genuinely laughing, the sound carrying across the grass. Meghan stood in the doorway watching them, feeling something she hadn't felt in years. Not peace exactly. But presence. Being here, in this moment, with these people she loved, without the weight of tomorrow crushing them.

The garden was warm. Her children were laughing. Her husband was present. And that, finally, was enough.

"Nobody cares about them anymore"
Piers Morgan, Sky News Australia, 16 September 2021

12

'Recollections May Vary'

The photograph sits in a frame on the bookshelf, half-hidden behind newer pictures but still there, still visible if you know to look. Windsor Castle, May 2018. Meghan in white, Harry beside her, the carriage ride through crowds that seemed to stretch forever. She looks young in the photo. Not in years, she was 36, but in something else. Hope, maybe. The kind that comes before you understand what it could cost you.

She doesn't look at the photo often. Not because it hurts, though sometimes it does, but because the woman in that frame feels like someone she knew once rather than someone she was. The distance between that day and this one isn't measurable in years alone. It's measured in everything she learned about institutions, about herself, about the difference between belonging somewhere and being allowed to exist there.

Five years have passed since they left Britain. Long enough that California feels like home in ways London never did. Long enough that Archie's British accent has softened into something more American, though he code-switches when talking to his father's family on the phone. Long enough that Lilibet has never known any other life, no comparison point for the life they've built here. To her, this is simply life. Normal, uncomplicated by history she's too young to carry. When Charles became King in September 2022, both children technically became prince and princess, entitled to HRH status by the rules George V established in 1917. The palace website was slow to update their titles, eventually listing them without the HRH styling.

The morning routine is ordinary in ways that still feel remarkable. Archie needs breakfast, his preferences changing daily in the way of children who've just discovered opinions. Today it's pancakes, but only if they're shaped like bears. Yesterday it was toast with peanut butter, but not cut into triangles. The day before, nothing would do except cereal from the blue bowl, and Meghan had spent ten minutes searching for the blue bowl while he stood in the kitchen doorway, patient and immovable. Lilibet wants to be held while Meghan makes coffee, her small weight familiar against Meghan's hip, her fingers reaching for everything within grasp. At two, she has opinions about the world that she expresses with the certainty of someone who has never been wrong. "No Archie," she'll say when her brother does something she disapproves of, her voice carrying the authority of a tiny monarch. The irony is not lost on her parents. Harry is outside already, checking something in the garden, his silhouette visible through the kitchen window. The house smells like toast and the particular chaos of family mornings. Nothing about it is royal. Everything about it is theirs.

Meghan has stopped counting the days since they left London. Time has settled from calendar to rhythm, from dates to seasons marked by children's growth rather than palace obligations. Archie has started school, a small private place where no one treats him differently, where his surname matters less than his ability to share toys. He came home one day talking about a friend named

Marco who had the best fruit snacks and knew all the dinosaur names. He hadn't mentioned anything about Marco's parents being impressed by his lineage. He hadn't mentioned lineage at all. He'd mentioned fruit snacks. Meghan counted this as victory. Lilibet is talking now, full sentences that delight and occasionally terrify her parents with their directness. Life has texture again. Mundane, complicated, exhausting texture that feels like privilege after years of everything being performance.

The garden has grown since they moved in. Tomatoes in raised beds, their skins splitting in the California heat when Meghan forgets to water them. Basil that spreads faster than she can use it, lemon verbena that scents her hands when she brushes past, mint that has escaped its container and colonised a corner near the fence. She planted a lemon tree their first spring, a small thing barely taller than Archie, and watched it struggle through summer drought and then suddenly flourish, putting out leaves and then flowers and then actual lemons that Meghan picked with absurd pride, as if she'd done something more than plant it in the right spot and remember to water it most of the time. She's discovered she likes working with soil, the immediate feedback of planting something and watching it respond. Saturday mornings, while Harry makes breakfast, she weeds and waters and harvests whatever is ready. The children follow her sometimes, Archie helping dig holes for new seedlings, his small trowel moving dirt with focused concentration. Lilibet picks tomatoes regardless of whether they're ripe, presenting green ones to Meghan with the expectation of praise. Meghan gives it. The gardening lesson can come later. The garden doesn't care about narratives or public opinion. It grows if you water it. It withers if you don't.

Harry has taken to cooking. Not elaborately, nothing that would end up in magazines, but competently. Pasta that doesn't burn. Chicken that's actually cooked through. Vegetables roasted with olive oil and whatever herbs the garden offers. He makes a risotto now that Meghan genuinely loves, standing at the stove stirring for forty minutes while she keeps the children occupied, the smell of saffron filling the kitchen. He makes a roast chicken on Sundays that they've started calling "the chicken," as in, "Should we do the chicken this weekend?" It involves lemon and garlic and some technique he learnt from a YouTube video, and the children fight over who gets the crispy skin bits. They eat dinner together most nights, phones put away, just family around a table talking about small things. What Archie learned at school. What Lilibet discovered about gravity by dropping her food repeatedly. Whether the fence needs repairing. Domestic concerns that feel almost ridiculously normal given where they've been.

But normal was the goal. Not obscurity, they've accepted that obscurity is impossible. But ordinary life lived extraordinarily publicly rather than extraordinary life lived ordinarily. They can take their children to the beach without security forming cordons. The first time they went to Santa Barbara beach as a family, Archie was barely four, still learning to trust that the sand wouldn't swallow him, that the waves would always pull back. Meghan sat beside him at the tide line, building a wall that would inevitably fall, rebuilding it, letting him feel the rhythm of attempt and collapse and attempt again. Harry and Lilibet were further up the beach, Lilibet in her sun hat, pointing at seagulls with the intensity of someone conducting an inventory. "Bird," she announced. "Bird. Bird. More bird." Harry confirmed each sighting with matching solemnity. They stayed until sunset that day, until the children were sandy and tired and happy, until the beach had emptied and they were just another family packing up towels and sand toys. No photographs appeared. No headlines followed. They went home and bathed the children and collapsed on the sofa with wine, marvelling at the ordinariness of it all.

Now beach trips are routine. Saturday afternoons when the weather cooperates, which in California means most Saturdays. They pack a cooler with sandwiches and fruit, bring buckets and spades and the inflatable ball that always ends up in the water. Archie has learnt to bodyboard in the small waves, throwing himself onto the foam with the fearlessness of a child who hasn't yet learnt that the ocean can hurt you. Lilibet prefers the sand, building structures that have no identifiable shape but which she defends fiercely from the incoming tide. Meghan reads sometimes, or pretends to, her eyes lifting from the page every few seconds to track her children, to make sure Archie's head is still above water, to make sure Lilibet hasn't decided to eat the sand she's playing with. Harry bodysurfs alongside Archie, the two of them laughing at wipeouts, competing to catch the biggest wave. These afternoons feel like gifts. Simple, unremarkable, irreplaceable.

They can go to the farmers market without photographers turning shopping into headlines. Sunday mornings in Montecito, the four of them moving between stalls, Archie examining fruit with the seriousness of a produce inspector, Lilibet strapped to Harry's chest, her eyes wide at the colours and sounds. There's a bread vendor Meghan likes, an older woman who makes sourdough that's chewy and sour in exactly the right proportions. There's a flower stall where Archie picks out sunflowers for the kitchen table, always sunflowers, because they're tall and yellow and "look happy, Mum." There's a coffee cart where Harry gets his flat white and Meghan gets something complicated with oat milk that she'd be embarrassed to order in front of anyone who knew her in her London days. The vendor who recognises them doesn't mention it, just hands over the loaf and says something about the weather. California has absorbed them in ways London never could, treating fame as unremarkable, treating their presence as just another data point in a city full of people who'd been other things before they were here.

Lilibet at two is different from Archie at two. Where he was watchful and quiet, she is loud and certain. Where he measured new situations carefully before engaging, she charges in head-first, assuming the world will accommodate her. She has her father's red hair, bright copper in certain light, and her mother's directness, a combination that already suggests interesting teenage years ahead. She wants what she wants when she wants it, and the concept of waiting or compromise has not yet entered her vocabulary. She follows her brother everywhere, imitating his games, claiming his toys, inserting herself into whatever he's doing with the confidence of someone who has never been told no. Archie tolerates this with the resigned patience of older siblings everywhere. Sometimes he complains. Mostly he just moves over and makes room. "Lili, you can be the dinosaur helper," he'll say, adapting his games to include her, even when her help consists mostly of knocking things over.

She has rituals already, small routines that she insists upon with the inflexibility of a child discovering the comfort of predictability. The same sippy cup every morning. The same goodnight book, the one with the rabbit, read twice because once is never sufficient. Her blanket must come to the table at meals, must travel in the car, must be within reach at all times. She calls it "Bee" for reasons nobody can explain, since it has no bees on it, just a pattern of stars. The attachment is fierce and non-negotiable. One evening, when Bee couldn't be found, she cried with such genuine devastation that Harry turned the house upside down for forty minutes before discovering it wedged behind the sofa. The relief on her face when he presented it was comic and also moving, the intensity of her feelings untempered by adult awareness that things could be replaced, that loss could be survived.

One afternoon, Meghan watches them playing in the garden, Archie explaining something complicated about dinosaurs while Lilibet listens with apparent attention. The explanation involves hand gestures and sound effects and a level of paleontological detail that suggests Harry's been reading to him from books aimed at much older children. Lilibet nods seriously at each point, then turns to Meghan and says, "More juice please." She hasn't understood a word. But she's participated, been included, been part of something with her brother. That's what matters to her. Meghan brings the juice and sits on the grass beside them, the California sun warm on her face, her children's voices carrying over the sound of bees in the lavender.

Archewell has taken shape slowly, deliberately, built with intention rather than speed. They fund organisations supporting women's leadership, mental health initiatives, media literacy programs. The kind of work Meghan had cared about before she'd become duchess, before survival had consumed all available bandwidth.

One afternoon, Meghan visits a women's shelter Archewell supports, bringing supplies but mostly just listening to stories from women rebuilding lives after violence, after loss, after systems had failed them repeatedly. One woman, late forties, asks Meghan how she'd survived the press attacks.

"I had help," Meghan says honestly. "My husband. My mother. Friends who didn't need me to be perfect. And I gave myself permission to not be okay sometimes."

The woman nods thoughtfully. "That last part's the hardest."

"It is. But it's also the most important."

Driving home, Meghan thinks about that conversation. How strange it is to be offering advice about surviving scrutiny when she still doesn't feel entirely sure she has survived, or if survival is ongoing rather than completed.

The creative work has come back gradually. The podcast was her first return to public-facing creative work. *Archetypes*, conversations with women about labels that limited them, stereotypes that shaped perception. She'd interviewed people she admired, asked questions that interested her, created content that reflected her actual curiosity rather than what some focus group thought would sell. The recording studio became a space she looked forward to entering, headphones on, microphone in front of her, conversations unfolding in real time. The technical aspects took adjustment, learning to speak differently for audio than for video, learning to trust pauses that felt endless but sounded natural, learning that the best conversations happened when she forgot the microphone was there at all.

The Serena Williams episode had been challenging to put together. They'd been friends for years, but friendship and interview are different things, require different muscles. Meghan spent weeks thinking about what she wanted to ask, what she wanted to explore, what the word "ambitious" meant when applied to women and why it carried weight it didn't carry for men. She wrote questions and discarded them, talked through ideas with Harry at dinner, worried that she'd ask the wrong thing or push too hard or not push enough. In the studio, Serena was funny and honest and unguarded in ways that made the conversation feel like catching up rather than recording. They talked about motherhood, about pressure, about bodies that belonged to themselves rather than to public opinion. Serena said something about ambition being treated as a dirty word for women, about how wanting things was somehow suspect when you were female. "Men with ambition are leaders," she said. "Women with ambition are problems." Meghan felt the truth of it land in her chest, familiar and infuriating. She thought about every time she'd been called difficult, demanding, too much. She thought about the emails at 5am that had been evidence of pathology rather than dedication. She thought about the years she'd spent trying to want less, be less, take up less space.

Mariah Carey's episode went in unexpected directions. They'd planned to discuss diva, the word and its implications, the way it was used to diminish and control. But the conversation wandered into childhood, into being biracial, into the particular loneliness of not fitting neatly into categories. Mariah talked about feeling not enough of anything, too much of everything, never quite belonging wherever she was. She described looking at forms with boxes to tick and never knowing which box was hers. Meghan recognised every word. She'd lived it. Was still living it, in different contexts. They ended up talking for three hours, only some of which made the final edit. The parts that didn't make it were sometimes the most meaningful, the tangents and confessions and shared recognitions that didn't fit the episode's theme but that stayed with Meghan long after the recording ended.

Each episode required something different. Gloria Steinem wanted to discuss power structures and systemic change, and Meghan found herself learning as much as leading, trying to keep up with a mind that had been analysing these systems for decades. Paris Hilton wanted to discuss media construction and the gap between image and reality, and Meghan felt unexpected kinship with someone whose public persona bore so little resemblance to the person sitting across from her. Mindy Kaling wanted to discuss comedy and motherhood and the freedom that came with not caring what people thought. Meghan found herself energised by the conversations, by the process of asking questions and actually listening to answers rather than waiting for her turn to speak. This was what she'd missed about work. The engagement. The purpose. The sense of building something that might matter to someone somewhere.

The Spotify deal collapsed in June 2023. The podcast had run for one season, twelve episodes, conversations Meghan was proud of. But Spotify wanted more content, faster production, different focus. The creative differences became irreconcilable. The partnership ended by mutual agreement, both sides releasing diplomatic statements about different priorities.

Bill Simmons, a Spotify executive, called them "fucking grifters" on his podcast days later. The comment went viral immediately. Meghan read it sitting at her desk, the words sharp and personal in ways professional criticism usually wasn't. Grifters. Con artists. People who'd taken Spotify's money without delivering value.

She'd delivered twelve episodes. Interviews with Serena Williams, Mariah Carey, Mindy Kaling, experts discussing historical context, production quality that matched any other major podcast. But because the deal ended early, because Spotify had expected more, she was a grifter.

"It's not worth responding to," Harry said when she showed him the comment.

"I know but I want people to understand what really happened."

"They won't. They've decided we're the villains. Facts don't matter to people who've made up their minds."

She's also started writing. Not memoir, she's lived that story publicly enough. But essays, pieces that explore themes from her experience without making the experience the centre. Identity, belonging, the cost of authenticity in systems designed to reward performance. The writing is harder than acting ever was, requiring different vulnerability, different precision. But it's hers in ways that feel important. She writes in the morning, before the children wake, coffee beside her, the house quiet. Sometimes the words come easily, paragraphs appearing as if dictated from somewhere outside herself. More often they don't. She'll spend an hour on a single sentence, trying to make it say exactly what she means without saying too much, without saying too little. But the practice of returning to the page, of trying again, of building something sentence by sentence, feels like reclaiming a part of herself she'd lost somewhere between Toronto and London.

Harry works on content about mental health, about veterans, about the specific loneliness of growing up in public. His perspective has value precisely because he's lived it, understood it from inside rather than as academic exercise.

One evening, reviewing footage for an upcoming project, Meghan watches herself on screen and feels the familiar dissociation of seeing your face as object rather than mirror. The woman talking looks confident, articulate, present. The woman watching feels tired, uncertain, still processing everything that had brought her to this chair in this office in this California house. Both women are real. Both women are her. The gap between external presentation and internal experience has narrowed but never closed.

Motherhood has changed everything and nothing. Archie and Lilibet don't care about headlines or history. They care about snacks and stories and whether their parents will play whatever game they've just invented. Meghan finds relief in their indifference to everything except immediate experience. She can be just Mom. Not former duchess, not controversial figure, not any of the labels that had been applied without her consent. Just the person who makes breakfast and enforces bedtimes and reads books with silly voices.

But she's also shaping how they'll understand themselves eventually. Both children are biracial. Both will grow up knowing their grandmother had been princess, their grandfather is king, their father had been prince. Both will have to navigate identity in ways that are complicated by circumstances beyond their control. Meghan wants to give them tools she'd had to find herself. Permission to be multiple things simultaneously. Confidence in their own perception when the world tries to tell them otherwise. The understanding that you can love people and still leave situations that hurt you.

Archie is old enough now to ask questions about why he has a title he doesn't use, why some kids at school know who his grandmother is, why their family sometimes appears in news that other families don't. Meghan answers honestly, age-appropriately, trying to give him truth without burden.

"Your father's family is very old and very famous," she explains once. "That means people are interested in them, in us. It doesn't mean anything about who you are. You're just Archie, and that's more than enough."

"But why don't we live near them? Like other families?"

"Because sometimes families live in different places. And that's okay. We still love them. We just love them from here."

He seems to accept this, the way children accept information that makes sense within their limited context. Later, when he's older, there will be harder questions. Why did you leave? Why don't we see them more? What happened? She'll answer those too, as honestly as she can without making him carry adult complexity.

Lilibet is still young enough that her questions are simpler. Why is the sky blue? Where do birds sleep? Can I have another biscuit? Meghan cherishes the simplicity, knowing it won't last, that eventually her daughter too will need explanations for family geography that doesn't match the model she sees around her.

Her mother visits often, the drive from Los Angeles manageable enough for regular dinners, for afternoons with grandchildren who adore her. Doria arrives with tupperware containers of food Meghan hasn't asked for but always needs, with books she thinks the children will like, with the quiet presence of someone who doesn't require entertainment. She sits on the floor with Archie building Lego structures that eventually get destroyed by Lilibet's determined small hands. She reads to Lilibet in a voice that makes the little girl go still with attention, thumb in mouth, eyes fixed on her grandmother's face. Doria teaches them songs Meghan remembers from her own childhood, simple melodies about sunshine and rain and loving someone forever. Sometimes, watching her mother with her children, Meghan feels the generations connect, feels herself as a link in a chain that stretches backward and forward in ways she couldn't have imagined when she was young and thinking only of her own future. Doria has watched Meghan survive impossible things with the steady faith of someone who'd known her daughter would survive because she'd raised her to. Now she watches her granddaughter and grandson with the same quiet confidence, trusting they'll be okay because they come from people who'd learned how to be okay despite everything.

"You're doing good, baby," Doria says one afternoon, watching Meghan referee a dispute between Archie and Lilibet over who gets the blue cup.

"I'm tired," Meghan admits.

"Tired and good aren't mutually exclusive."

Meghan laughs despite herself. "Is that your wisdom for the day?"

"That's my wisdom for your whole life. You can be exhausted and still be doing fine."

The friends they've made in California are different from palace acquaintances. Real relationships built on actual compatibility rather than proximity to power. People who'd been famous themselves and understood the particular exhaustion of public life. Others who'd never been famous and didn't care about their titles or history. Artists, activists, parents struggling with the same ordinary problems everyone struggles with. School decisions. Work-life balance. How to raise decent humans in an indecent world.

One couple they've grown close to has teenage children. The daughter, 16, tells Meghan once that she'd read about everything that happened in London.

"Do you regret it?" the girl asks. "Getting married, I mean. Given everything that came after."

Meghan thinks about the question. She's asked herself variations countless times. "I regret what the institution did. I don't regret loving Harry. And I definitely don't regret my children existing."

"But you lost a lot."

"I did. But I also found out who I actually was underneath all the versions of myself I'd been performing. There's value in that, even when it's painful."

The girl seems to absorb this. "I think that's brave."

"I think it was necessary. Bravery is when you have a choice. I just did what I had to do to survive."

Later, telling Harry about the conversation, he smiles slightly. "You really don't see it, do you?"

"See what?"

"That survival was the brave choice. You could have stayed and diminished yourself. Could have made it work by making yourself smaller. You chose not to. That's brave."

She kisses him, grateful for his perspective even when she can't quite internalise it.

The relationship with Harry's family remains complicated. Charles sends birthday cards to the grandchildren. William's family sends Christmas gifts. There are phone calls on significant occasions, brief and careful, everyone performing civility without attempting depth. The rift hasn't healed. But it has stopped bleeding, which is progress of a sort.

Meghan has released the hope of reconciliation without quite giving up on it. A subtle distinction, but important. She doesn't wait for apologies that might never come. She doesn't hold her breath for the family to acknowledge what had happened, how the system had failed, what their silence had cost. But if someday they reached out genuinely, she'd consider responding. The door isn't open, but it isn't welded shut either.

Harry struggles more with the separation. He loves his family despite everything, loves them in the complicated way you love people who've hurt you but whom you can't stop caring about. He speaks to his father occasionally, conversations that leave him quiet afterwards, processing what had been said and what remained unsaid. William is harder. The brotherly closeness they'd shared is gone, replaced by polite distance that feels more permanent than temporary anger.

"Do you think they'll ever understand why we left?" Harry asks one evening, after a particularly stilted phone call with his father. Meghan thinks about her answer.

"I think they understand the facts. I don't think they'll ever understand the feeling. You can't explain drowning to someone who's never been underwater."

He nods slowly. "That's what makes it lonely. They think we left over headlines. They don't understand we left to survive."

She takes his hand, squeezes it. There is nothing else to say. Some gaps can't be bridged with words.

One afternoon, sorting through old papers, Meghan finds a journal from her Toronto years. Before Harry. Before everything. She reads entries about auditions, about advocacy work, about hopes for the future that were simultaneously modest and vast. The woman writing those entries wanted to matter, wanted her work to mean something, wanted to use whatever platform she achieved for purposes beyond herself.

Reading it, Meghan feels strange recognition. She'd achieved the platform. Just not the way she'd imagined. And the cost had been higher than any version of her could have anticipated. But the core remains. She still wants her work to matter. She still wants to use her voice for purposes beyond herself. The mechanism has changed. The foundation hasn't.

She thinks about that younger self, the woman boarding planes to Rwanda, writing posts for *The Tig*, believing earnestly that you could change systems from inside if you just worked hard enough, if you just maintained integrity. She wants to tell that woman she'd been right about some things, wrong about others, and that the wrongness wouldn't invalidate the rightness.

But mostly, she wants to tell her that she'd survive. That the worst parts wouldn't break her, even when breaking felt inevitable. That she'd find her way to something like peace, even if peace looked different than expected. That the story didn't end with the palace. It just changed chapters.

There are moments now that feel like joy rather than just survival. Saturday afternoon in the garden, Harry teaching Archie to kick a football while Lilibet picks flowers she isn't supposed to pick, presenting them to Meghan with the solemnity of a gift. The four of them in the kitchen making pizza, flour everywhere, Lilibet eating cheese directly from the bag while Archie arranges pepperoni in careful patterns and Harry kneads dough with more enthusiasm than technique. Evening walks around the neighbourhood, Archie on his bicycle, Lilibet in the stroller, the sun setting over the mountains in colours that look fake but aren't. Dance parties in the living room, music too loud, everyone moving in ways that would embarrass them if anyone were watching, Lilibet stomping in circles while Archie attempts moves he's seen on television. These moments accumulate. They become the texture of life.

One Saturday, they take the children hiking. A gentle trail, nothing ambitious, just family moving through trees without destination beyond moving. Archie runs ahead, turning back frequently to make sure they're following. Lilibet rides on Harry's shoulders, her small hands gripping his hair. Meghan walks beside them, breathing air that smells like eucalyptus and dirt and the particular scent of California summer.

At the trail's peak, they stop to drink water, to look at the view stretching toward the ocean. The landscape is beautiful in ways that never get old. Gold hills, blue sky, distance that feels like possibility rather than distance.

"This is good," Harry says quietly.

Meghan nods. "This is good."

They don't need to elaborate. After everything, good is enough. Better than enough. Good is the goal they'd been reaching for without quite believing it was achievable. And here it is. Not perfect. Not uncomplicated. Not without its own challenges and frustrations. Just good.

Back home that evening, after children are bathed and storied and finally, blessedly asleep, Meghan stands on their bedroom balcony looking at stars. Harry comes out to join her, two glasses of wine in hand. They stand in comfortable silence, the kind that only comes after surviving things together.

"Do you miss it?" he asks eventually. "Any of it?"

Meghan considers the question honestly. "I miss the possibility of what it could have been. Before I understood what it was."

"That's not the same as missing it."

"No. It's not."

"Do you have regrets?"

She turns to look at him. "I regret that loving you cost us both so much. I don't regret loving you."

He pulls her closer, his arm around her shoulders.

"I'd choose you again. Every time."

"Even knowing what it would cost?"

"Especially! The cost of not choosing you would have been losing myself entirely."

They stand like that, holding each other in the California night, two people who'd survived a war and are learning how to live in peacetime. The scars remain. Some days hurt more than others. But they are here, whole enough, together.

Meghan looks at the photograph one more time. The young woman in white, waving from a carriage, believing she was beginning something. She had been. Just not what she'd imagined. No fairy tale or modernising force inside an ancient institution. But a journey toward understanding who she actually was beneath all the versions of herself she'd performed.

That journey had cost everything. And given her everything. Both things are true simultaneously.

She closes the journal, puts it back on the shelf beside the photograph. Behind her, the house hums with life. Harry is reading to the children, their voices carrying down the hallway. Dinner needs preparing. Laundry needs folding. Life needs living.

She walks toward those voices, toward the ordinary extraordinary future waiting in the next room. The palace is behind her. The story the world tells about her will continue, but it no longer has the power to define her.

She is Meghan. Not duchess, not former anything, just herself. Whole, complicated, imperfect, and enough.

And that, finally, is the ending she'd been trying to find.

Not the one she'd planned.

But the one she'd survived to claim.

The one that is hers.

> **"Whilst some recollections may vary,
> they are taken very seriously"**
> Buckingham Palace statement, 9 March 2021

Notes on Sources

This biography is constructed from public record, including court documents, broadcast interviews, published memoirs, contemporaneous journalism, and official statements. Where dialogue appears, it is based on the subjects' own accounts, legal testimony, or documented reporting. In cases where accounts conflict, the version best supported by available evidence is presented.

Primary Sources

The book draws extensively from Meghan and Harry's own words. The March 2021 *CBS* interview with Oprah Winfrey provides the most comprehensive account of Meghan's mental health crisis, the conversations about Archie's skin colour, and palace failures to protect her. The 2022 *Netflix* documentary *Harry & Meghan* (six episodes) offers detailed chronological testimony about their courtship, media treatment, and decision to leave, including previously unseen personal footage and contemporaneous text messages. Prince Harry's 2023 memoir *Spare* provides essential context on his childhood trauma, his relationship with William, and his perspective on institutional dysfunction. These three sources form the evidential backbone of this biography. Earlier interviews given before and during their time as working royals provide additional context.

Journalism & Media Coverage

British and American journalism is used both as source material and as subject. Tabloid coverage is referenced to illustrate pattern and rhetoric rather than to establish fact. Long-form investigative journalism from outlets including *The Guardian, The New York Times, The Atlantic,* and the *London Review of Books* provides essential context. Palace statements and press releases are treated as institutional communications serving reputational interests rather than neutral historical record. Where conflicting accounts exist, particularly regarding staff departures, family relationships, and private conversations, I have weighed credibility based on documentation, consistency, and who had reputational interest in which version.

Secondary Sources

Published biographies and analyses of the royal family provide historical context and institutional understanding, though these are weighted according to author access, bias, and timing. Works by Valentine Low, Tina Brown, Omid Scobie and Carolyn Durand, and others offer perspectives shaped by their relationships with palace sources or the Sussexes respectively. All are used critically, with awareness of their limitations.

Limitations

No biography of living subjects can be complete or final. This account ends in late 2023; the story continues to unfold. I have attempted to present Meghan's experiences with fairness and factual accuracy while acknowledging that institutional narratives and personal narratives often diverge irreconcilably. Where possible, I have let events speak for themselves rather than imposing interpretation. Readers seeking a defence of the monarchy or an uncritical celebration of the Sussexes will find neither here. The aim is understanding, not verdict.

Bibliography

Books
Brown, Tina. *The Palace Papers: Inside the House of Windsor, the Truth and the Turmoil*. New York: Crown, 2022.

Harry, Duke of Sussex. *Spare*. London: Bantam Press, 2023.

Low, Valentine. *Courtiers: The Hidden Power Behind the Crown*. London: Headline, 2022.

Maclaran, Pauline. *Royal Fever: The British Monarchy in Consumer Culture*. Oakland: University of California Press, 2020.

Scobie, Omid, and Carolyn Durand. *Finding Freedom: Harry and Meghan and the Making of a Modern Royal Family*. London: HarperCollins, 2020.

Scobie, Omid. *Endgame: Inside the Royal Family and the Monarchy's Fight for Survival*. London: HarperCollins, 2023.

Legal Documents
Markle v. Associated Newspapers Ltd [2021] EWHC 273 (Ch). High Court of Justice, Chancery Division, 11 February 2021.

Phone hacking litigation: *Various Claimants v. News Group Newspapers Ltd* and related proceedings, 2019-2023.

Broadcast Interviews & Documentaries
BBC News. "Prince Harry and Meghan Markle: The Engagement Interview." 27 November 2017.

Garbus, Liz, dir. *Harry & Meghan*. Netflix, 2022.

Winfrey, Oprah. *Oprah with Meghan and Harry: A CBS Primetime Special*. CBS, 7 March 2021.

Official Statements & Public Records
Buckingham Palace. "Statement on the Duke and Duchess of Sussex." 18 January 2020.

Buckingham Palace. "Statement in Response to Interview." 9 March 2021.

Kensington Palace. "Statement on Harassment and Abuse." 8 November 2016.

Ofcom. "Broadcast and On Demand Bulletin, Issue 428." 1 March 2021. Investigation into *ITV*'s *Good Morning Britain* (57,121 complaints), complaint reference CAS-62026-B7V2Z1.

Journalism & Media Analysis
Extensive reporting from *Associated Press, BBC News, The Guardian, The Independent, The New York Times, Reuters, The Telegraph*. Long-form analysis from *The Atlantic, London Review of Books, New Statesman, Vanity Fair*. Selected tabloid coverage from *Daily Mail, The Sun,* and *Mail on Sunday* cited for illustrative and contextual purposes.

UN & Institutional Records
UN Women. "Gender Equality In Political Participation" speech by Meghan Markle, 8 March 2015.

Various public speeches and appearances, 2015-2023.

Author's Note

As this book went to press in January 2026, Prince Harry gave emotional testimony in the High Court against Associated Newspapers Limited, stating that the publisher had 'made my wife's life an absolute misery.' His evidence corroborates the experiences documented in these pages.

About the Author

A writer, artist and researcher focused on people, media and power, Rowan Lowry lives and works in Glasgow, and has two children. The author would like to thank Lise Smith for her thorough research and fact-checking, and Roxanne 'Red Pen' Donatello for the editorial polish.